The Chamberlain Selection of

NEW ENGLAND ROOMS

1639–1863

The Chamberlain Selection of
New

England

ROOMS

1639-1863

BY SAMUEL CHAMBERLAIN and
NARCISSA G. CHAMBERLAIN

HASTINGS HOUSE,   PUBLISHERS   *NEW YORK*

PUBLISHED 1972 BY HASTINGS HOUSE, PUBLISHERS, INC.

ALL RIGHTS RESERVED

INCLUDING THE RIGHT OF REPRODUCTION

IN WHOLE OR IN PART IN ANY FORM

PUBLISHED SIMULTANEOUSLY IN CANADA

BY S. J. REGINALD SAUNDERS & CO., LTD., TORONTO 2B

DON MILLS, ONTARIO

PRODUCED IN COLLABORATION WITH CHANTICLEER PRESS, INC., NEW YORK

PRINTED BY CONZETT & HUBER, ZURICH, SWITZERLAND

Library of Congress Cataloging in Publication Data

Chamberlain Samuel, date
    The Chamberlain selection of New England rooms, 1639–1863.

    1. Interior decoration—New England. 2. New England—Historic
houses, etc. I. Chamberlain, Narcissa G., joint author. II. Title.

NK 2005.C45   917.4   72–6160
ISBN 0–8038–1176–4

CONTENTS

Foreword 7

FOREWORD

New England, in area only a small northeastern segment of the United States, makes up for its modest size in other ways. Historically, the land that includes Plymouth and Lexington is significant as the setting of the early colonization of America and its later struggle for freedom. From the viewpoint of natural beauty, the six New England states possess an abundant ecological bounty, from the coast of Maine to the green hills of Vermont. The traveling public is attracted in ever-increasing numbers to these hospitable states, whose lakes and shores are lined with opportunities for a summer vacation, and whose wintry hills offer a version of paradise to today's exuberant generation of skiers.

But there are other interests for quieter tastes. A New England village is one of them. Serene in its rural setting with a white church and old houses on the green, and a country inn with good Yankee food, it appears in scores of variations to tempt more romantic travelers from other states and from abroad. The architectural heritage of this small region is disproportionately rich. From Bulfinch to Richardson, great designers have left their marks on Boston, Hartford, Providence and other cities. College campuses and seasoned preparatory schools often reveal Colonial architecture of impeccable taste. Few buildings are more gratifying than a well-designed village church or town hall. Most rewarding of all, in the opinion of many visitors, are the houses that the early New Englanders have built for themselves. Nothing else gives as revealing a picture of their way of life, their architectural good sense, and their discriminating taste in furniture and décor. Much of the romance and the drama of our history is expressed in these very personal insights into the lives of our earlier citizens.

Obviously an imposing number of books have been written on all these aspects of New England—its history, natural beauty and architectural achievement. The bibliography of volumes on its houses of the past is perhaps less complete, and seems to offer an opening for another book on the more intimate theme of historic interiors. This is a subject that happily can be shared with visitors and students of antiquity, for a great many of the houses illustrated in this book are open to the public during the summer months, and often longer. This hospitable state of affairs is due to a variety of organizations, the most usual one being the local historical society. Pride in a particular town mansion, or ancient seventeenth-century house is strong in these communities, and they have been restored, furnished with appropriate period pieces, and made available to

7

visitors. Ladies of the local historical society act as guides and hostesses, and emphasize the hospitable nature of their community. Sometimes local chapters of the Colonial Dames of America or the Daughters of the American Revolution maintain and show such houses. On a much larger scale is the remarkable Society for the Preservation of New England Antiquities, with headquarters in Boston, which is responsible for the rescue or maintenance of almost fifty houses throughout the Northeast. Most of these are open to visitors in summer, and a number of them are illustrated in these pages. These will be identified by the initials SPNEA. In Connecticut, another group effort is carried on by the Antiquarian and Landmarks Society, Inc., of Connecticut, four of whose houses are shown here. The Essex Institute in Salem, Massachusetts, is the owner of a few extraordinary buildings, among them two of the finest masterpieces of Samuel McIntire, the great carver-architect of Salem. Both of these are illustrated here. The Antiquarian House in Concord, Massachusetts, is an assemblage of historic rooms of various periods, all gathered under one roof. These appear in several places in this volume.

Finally, there are a few owners of private houses who have permitted us to photograph interiors to round out this selection. These remain anonymous. To them, as well as the historical societies and other generous organizations, we extend our appreciative thanks. A little of everything, as you can see, has been eligible in our selection of New England rooms, from 1639 to Victorian examples, and even a house that originated in Charleston, South Carolina. We hope that a certain vitality will be the result, and that monotony will be bypassed.

An approximate sequence in date is followed in presenting these houses, but this formula has not been rigidly maintained. Often a building includes several periods, the Royall House in Medford, Massachusetts, for example, and frequently the date is uncertain enough to demand a "circa".

About three hundred illustrations have been selected to tell an abbreviated story. These have been supplemented by captions which are often too restricted in space to do complete justice to their subject. To round out the picture, when necessary, the following notes are provided.

The subject of the development of New England taste is far from exhausted by this selection of fifty-six houses. Scores of other buildings of equal merit await the researcher. Restorations are under way in many places, and the interest in antiquity continues to mount. The New England of the past has a bright and definite future. The present selection illustrates the changing styles over more than two centuries and demonstrates the craftsmanship and good taste of our ancestors who produced it.

The oldest house in this selection, the HENRY WHITFIELD HOUSE (1639), is certainly one of the most exceptional *(Page 26)*. It was built by Henry Whitfield, an English vicar from Surrey, who migrated to Connecticut with twenty-five families of young people in 1639. They purchased a piece of land in what is now Guilford from the Squaw Sachem and immediately set to building a large house of stone, not taking advantage of the fact that wood was so plentiful. The walls were two feet thick, and the joists and rafters were husky hand-hewn oaken timbers. The style of the house resembles those found in the north of England. Its enormous fireplaces provided all the heat there was. This building was first of all a church, second a meeting hall, third a hostel for wayfarers and lastly a home for the Whitfields and seven of their nine children. It was far from a typical New England house. Once having established his congregation, the Reverend Mr. Whitfield sailed back to England in 1650 and never returned.

The ensuing years were unkind to the old stone house, as might be expected. Toward the end of the nineteenth century it had deteriorated badly and became the home of a Long Island trucker. First steps to rescue it were taken by the Connecticut Society of the Colonial Dames of America in 1897, and it was ultimately restored to its present condition under architect J. Frederick Kelly in 1937. Its furnishings today are a mixture of English and American pieces. It is open to the public from April 1st to October 31st.

The birth of the iron industry in America occurred in 1642 when the first crude forge was built at the head of an inlet in the village of Saugus, Massachusetts. At that time it bore the appropriate name of Hammersmith. In recent years a replica of the old ironworks has been designed and built by a firm of Boston architects. Today it is complete with waterwheels, smelters and furnaces, and is maintained for visitors by the National Park Service. In connection with this replica is a much older structure known as the IRONMASTER'S HOUSE, standing on a nearby rise of land *(Pages 27–30)*. It dates from the seventeenth century, and was built for Richard Leader, manager of the foundry. Tradition has it that the first models of the Pine Tree and Oak Tree shillings were made in this house. The ironworks employed over a hundred men, who had to be fed from time to time. This accounts for the presence of a large kitchen as well as a cooking fireplace in the Great Hall. This house was also a meeting place (the General Court is supposed to have met here) as well as a stopping place for travelers, who were given hospitality. The venerable dwelling has undergone many changes in succeeding years, and was restored by Wallace Nutting, photographer and antiquarian, in 1915. Some of the early furniture is his, and other period pieces were contributed by Mrs. Louise du Pont Crowninshield and others. The rooms show commendable restraint on the part of the restorers.

An accurate picture of prosperous New England family life in the seventeenth century is provided by the WHIPPLE HOUSE (1640) in Ipswich, Massachusetts, now handsomely restored, furnished and maintained by the Ipswich Historical Society *(Pages 31–32)*. The rooms are comfortable and inviting, roofed with beamed ceilings supported by massive chamfered summer beams. In front of the house is a charming herb and flower garden, stocked only with plants that thrived in the early days. In recent years, when it was proposed to repair the pitched roof of the Whipple House, the builders discovered evidence that two gables undoubtedly had graced the original structure. Today the house stands as it did in the beginning, with two fine Shakespearean gables.

The building that makes the greatest contribution to these pages is ANTIQUARIAN HOUSE in Concord, Massachusetts. At least eight times its various rooms have been illustrated, each from a different period. This is explained by the fact that the building is a fireproof brick shell built for a group of a dozen historic rooms owned by the Concord Antiquarian Society. It has the appearance of a comfortable country house. It all can be traced back to a town character, Cummings E. Davis, who had a passion for collecting antique furniture and anything else that was old, when nobody else did. At a moment when old pieces were being relegated to the attic, he would buy them cheaply or do odd chores to obtain them. Concord families would be glad to buy them back now at exalted prices. The old man wasn't quite all there, and used to exhibit his collection in a courthouse room, wearing a Colonial costume and a wig. Citizens of the town took pity, formed a Society and took over the collection, Davis included.

This was the beginning of Antiquarian House. The collection was first shown in the Reuben Brown House, but there was danger of fire, and a new fireproof building was built in 1929. Donations from many sources in Concord permitted the construction of this reposeful brick building with twelve period rooms dating from the seventeenth century to the Empire Room dated about 1825.

9

In addition to the period rooms there are two that recall two of Concord's vivid personalities, Henry Thoreau and Ralph Waldo Emerson. The hut at Walden Pond where Thoreau wrote and dreamed is reproduced with his meagre belongings. Emerson's study has been copied from the original in the Emerson House nearby. The entire contents of his study—books, portfolio, papers and furniture has been moved to this safe setting. Needless to say, many pilgrims come to Concord for this room alone. Of New England's many treasures, few houses can appeal to the lover of antiques as much as this, and we cannot recommend it highly enough.

The history of the TRISTRAM COFFIN HOUSE (1651), in Old Newbury, Massachusetts *(Page 37)*, is unusual in that it has been inhabited or owned by seven generations of the family, from Tristram Coffin, Jr. who probably acquired it when he married in 1653, to the sixth direct descendant, Joshua Coffin, scholar and historian, who died there in 1864 after having written the history of Newbury. It came into the hands of cousins who arranged to turn it over to the SPNEA in 1929. This was fortunate for the fascinating old structure, which has been added to time and again as children married and raised large families there. This unique old house is still in loving hands, and may be visited as a memorial to the Coffin family of Old Newbury.

The glory of the JOSHUA HEMPSTED HOUSE is truly its age *(Pages 38–40)*. The land grant was received in 1645. The house is the oldest structure in New London. It was built in 1678 by Joshua Hempsted on a generous and roomy scale, with small diamond-paned windows, now restored, and an extended frontal porch with a small chamber above the entry. Even the "new" part of the house, added by Joshua's grandson Nathanael, dates back to 1728. Nathanael's father, Joshua II, who was born and died in the house, kept a detailed and fascinating diary which recounts the history of the house and his own active life, an invaluable source for researchers. It now belongs to the New London County Historical Society. The house has been furnished with very early pieces, many of them of Hempsted family ownership, and is maintained by the Antiquarian and Landmarks Society, Inc., of Connecticut.

One of the most beautiful of New England villages, Farmington, Connecticut, is stately and patrician, a worthy setting for one of our most exclusive private schools for girls. Fine old eighteenth-century houses line the shaded streets, and the white village church shares the sloping green with the Library and Town Hall. The oldest house is probably the STANLEY-WHITMAN HOUSE *(Page 40)* built about 1660. It was restored in 1935 and deeded to the Farmington Village Green and Library Association, which maintains it as a museum. The house is built around a massive stone chimney, and has a pronounced frontal overhang adorned with decorative pendants, giving it a fine Elizabethan air. Two ground floor fireplaces were built into the chimney, one being the kitchen type with a vast broad lintel, and the other a more elaborate version with pilasters and carved moldings. We illustrate the latter.

The ancient community of Wethersfield, Connecticut had a frightening history of Indian massacres before settling down as a quiet farming town. Lieutenant John Buttolph, a Boston trader, liked its location on the Connecticut River and decided to try his luck in this outpost. This was in 1676. He succeeded both in business and in raising a large family. His heirs built the massive timbered BUTTOLPH-WILLIAMS HOUSE *(Pages 40–42)*, with a central stone chimney in about 1692. It had a few overhangs, typical of the Connecticut house of that time. Throughout the succeeding years it had many owners, but gradually fell into disrepair. The hurricane of 1938 gave it a final death blow. An enormous maple tree blew down and toppled on the roof, taking the chimney with it. Empty and forlorn, the old house was almost beseeching to be restored. In 1947 the work of rescue began, interrupted by delays and setbacks, but today the restoration is finished, under

10

expert supervision. It is correctly furnished with period pieces, and is open to the public under the ownership of the Antiquarian and Landmarks Society, Inc., of Connecticut.

The WHITE-ELLERY HOUSE is said to have been built by John White, pastor of the First Church in Gloucester, Massachusetts, in 1703 *(Pages 43–44)*. Some believe it to be even earlier, as there is evidence of a house having been built in this area in 1640. Whichever it may be, it is unusual as it seems to have been built complete, including the kitchen lean-to, all at one time. Usually such early houses were built part at a time, additional rooms and lean-to extensions being added later. The house was rescued and moved in 1947 to save it from the path of a concrete highway that was cut through the countryside. It is furnished with a wonderful collection of early furniture and household objects, and maintained by the Cape Ann Historical Association.

Together with the Antiquarian House in Concord, Massachusetts, BEAUPORT *(Page 45)*, is one of the most rewarding collections of period rooms in the country. It is an astonishing ensemble of interiors, each emphasizing a different phase of furniture and decoration. Its nationalities are varied—Jacobean English, Chinese, American Federal and seventeenth-century colonial. This assembling of treasures under one roof was accomplished by a celebrated decorator and architect, Henry Sleeper, between 1903 and 1934. His acquisitions were prodigal, and it took a great deal of space to house them. Thus you find rooms dedicated to Franklin, Shelly, Byron (with his own bed) and Nelson (with his own bedside lamp) and a Strawberry Hill Room reminiscent of Horace Walpole.

There is a circular tower for books. Classic prints are grouped on the walls. China and glass collections are abundant, and the French and English furniture makes an antiquarian's head swim. We recommend Beauport to our readers without reservation. It is located at Eastern Point, Massachusetts, an outpost of Gloucester, and is open to visitors during the summer months under the supervision of the SPNEA.

One of the most flawless examples of Elizabethan architecture on this continent is the PARSON CAPEN HOUSE *(Pages 46–47)*, built on a gentle knoll in Topsfield, Massachusetts. Constructed in 1683, it reflected its English ancestry, and may well have been built by artisans who had only recently sailed from the mother country.

Mr. Capen's bride, Priscilla, was a member of the prominent Appleton family, and she was not happy with the small parsonage offered by the town. This noble house with a steep roof, a conspicuous overhang on three sides, and a fine central chimney, was the result. In England it would probably have been a half-timbered edifice, but in Topsfield, clapboards were the solution for the outer surface. Inside its nail-studded door were sparse but congenial rooms, well furnished but free from frippery. The Parson died in 1725, and he lies buried beside his wife in a hillside burial plot near the old house, which was restored in 1914. The Topsfield Historical Society now takes good care of it, and welcomes visitors.

One of the most notable achievements of the SPNEA was the restoration of the ABRAHAM BROWNE, JR. HOUSE (*c.* 1690) in Watertown, Massachusetts, on the highway running west from Boston *(Pages 48–49)*. Great care was taken in this work, and there is photographic evidence to justify the restored seventeenth-century hall as it exists today. Few very early rooms can be called luxurious, but this comes close to it. It was here that a genuine three-part window frame was found, an apparently unique survivor. The furnishings of the great hall are truly convincing.

An authentic example of a Massachusetts farmhouse, home of a large family for two hundred and twenty-three years, TIME STONE FARM was first built in 1702 *(Pages 50–53)*. From this original, single, large room

11

with a stone chimney, the old house grew until it contained eleven rooms and as many fireplaces. In the garden is the sundial, or "time stone" which gave the place its name. The simple, informal antique furniture and household objects seem always to have been in these rooms, naturally acquired and used by a farming family throughout the years, though actually they are a collection gathered by the present owner in a lifetime.

The OGDEN HOUSE, an early Connecticut salt-box *(Pages 54–58)*, built originally by one David Ogden in the very early eighteenth century (probably prior to 1705) reached its present and completed form by two later additions built by the middle of the eighteenth century. It is said to have started as a two-room house on one side of the chimney, with the other two rooms, one above the other, being added by the next generation. The lean-to with its huge fireplace, was the last and completing element. Until recently the original three-foot, white pine shingles were still in place, with large rose-head nails to hold them. One finds here in the building itself and in the choice collection of antiques with which it is furnished, that aroma of authenticity and, at the same time, of mystery, that fills an ancient dwelling.

The BUBIER MANSION, a simple old central chimney house dating from about 1700, takes its name from an owner of French Channel Islands descent, whose heirs owned it until 1819 *(Pages 59–61)*. Originally of exposed beam construction, the posts and beams were boxed in and the paneling added probably about 1746. At that time Bubier acquired the other half of the house built against the same chimney by another family. The present restoration has been done with care, the original colors reproduced where possible. Most of the rooms have simple off-white plaster walls which set off the colorful painted woodwork to advantage, and form an excellent background for the collection of antiques with which the house is furnished.

The RICHARD WEBB HOUSE was built about 1700 and owned by the family and their heirs until 1882 *(Pages 62–65)*. As the surrounding countryside became urban and crowded, the old veteran was forced to retire, and was dismantled and fortunately stored and preserved until it could be put together again with loving care in another open location. It was furnished with choice pieces of seventeenth- and eighteenth-century furniture, and now glows with renewed life and warmth. The house is privately owned.

One of the prettiest delusions of early antiquarians in Massachusetts was that Anne Bradstreet, the first New England poetess and daughter-in-law of the Governor, lived in a fine old salt-box house in North Andover, Massachusetts. It had been assumed that the house was built for her after a fire that had destroyed an earlier dwelling. Recent studies of deeds have proven that it was actually built a quarter century after her death by the Reverend Thomas Barnard, pastor of the North Parish Church in Andover. As a dwelling of the first quarter of the eighteenth century, the PARSON BARNARD HOUSE (*c.* 1715) is an excellent example of the transitional style between the almost Elizabethan houses of the earlier century and the Georgian period that followed *(Pages 66–68)*. After Thomas Barnard's death his son John succeeded him in the ministry as well as owner of the house. The next pastor, William Symmes, purchased it from the heirs, and lived there until his death in 1807, leaving the house almost exactly as he had found it. The rooms have been furnished in styles suitable to the periods of the three first owners. There are choice pieces, many of them relating to these families or to the locality, that add authenticity to the setting. The old house is owned and maintained by the North Andover Historical Society.

The MACPHAEDRIS-WARNER HOUSE in Portsmouth, New Hampshire, a handsome brick structure, was built about 1716 by Archibald Macphaedris *(Pages 69–73)*. He married Sarah, the daughter of Lieutenant Governor John Wentworth, and sister of Benning Wentworth who later became Governor of the Province.

One of the descendants married Jonathan Warner of Portsmouth, who came to live in the house with his wife, thus lending his name also to the mansion. Although Governor Wentworth lived in the house for some years, he has not been so honored by posterity. Some of the features of this fine house, astonishingly elegant and sophisticated for its date in this provincial outpost, are three fully paneled rooms, one of which retains some of its original marbleizing, five eighteenth-century portraits of the Warner family by Joseph Blackburn, and some crude but interesting wall paintings in the stairway. The house is a Registered National Historic Landmark administered by the Warner House Association.

The CROWNINSHIELD-BENTLEY HOUSE, in Salem, Massachusetts *(Pages 75-79)*, was long the home of a distinguished Salem family, and for twenty-eight years the residence of their famous boarder, Dr. William Bentley, the celebrated clergyman-diarist. Consequently this house represents a rich slice of history. It has been well restored and furnished by the Essex Institute according to the several periods in which it was built, added to, and transformed. These stretch from 1727 when John Crowninshield acquired the land and presumably started building, until 1824, the date of the death of the widow Hannah Crowninshield, last member of the family to own it. Many Crowninshield possessions are found within the rooms, and the rest are mainly from Salem or Essex County. Dr. Bentley's lengthy diary, part gossip, part facts, and much of it a vivid description of the times, was a great source of inspiration in furnishing the house. His own room is so intensely personal in atmosphere that one almost sees him seated in the seventeenth-century arm chair which was his possession, or gazing with admiration at the engraved portrait of Thomas Jefferson, given to him by Jefferson himself.

A most interesting personality is tied up with an old red house in the open country near Middletown, Rhode Island *(Pages 80-81)*. It is called WHITEHALL, and was built in 1729 for George Berkeley, an outstanding cleric and Dean of Derry, in Ireland. Called the "Irish Plato", Berkeley was not quite forty-four when he landed in Newport in 1729. He had known Swift, Steele, Addison and Pope, and was a notable addition to the Newport community. He named his house Whitehall in loyalty to the English reigning family, whose palace bore that name. His stay in the Colonies was brief, and he returned in 1736 to England, giving his library of 880 volumes to Yale University. He also gave Whitehall to Yale, and the rent derived from it provided a scholarship known as "The Dean's Bounty". In later years Whitehall became a public house run by a Mr. Anthony, whose daughter became the mother of Gilbert Stuart, the great American portraitist.

British officers and men were quartered here during the Revolution. The old building is now maintained as an historical shrine by the Colonial Dames of America, and is open to the public in summer.

Old Newbury, Massachusetts, is a good stopover for antiquarians since it contains three fine old houses, all open to the public under the SPNEA. The most recent of the three is the SHORT HOUSE *(Page 82)*, dating from about 1733. This is a two-story wooden house built between ends of weathered brick, a most attractive combination. Its outstanding feature is the fine paneling to be found in two of the rooms. The paint has been removed from the wood, revealing sharp and skillful carving.

Along the old Post Road in affluent Greenwich, Connecticut, is a vivid reminder of Revolutionary days called PUTNAM COTTAGE *(Page 83)*. It is a fine old tavern built in 1731, faced with long whitewashed shingles, and sheltered by a wide front porch. General Israel Putnam was shaving in his room in this tavern on a February morning in 1779 when he caught the image of a Redcoat in his mirror. Losing no time, the General rushed out to his horse and plunged down a near-precipice which his pursuers were reluctant to

13

tackle. A bullet hit his hat, but he was uninjured and sped on to Stamford where he gathered reinforcements and returned to capture fifty Britishers. The former tavern has been restored and is open to the public under the auspices of the Putnam Hill Chapter, Daughters of the American Revolution. The newly rehabilitated stone fireplaces are items of major interest.

One of the most beautiful towns in the Berkshire Hills of Massachusetts is Stockbridge, a well-manicured community with a wide, grass-bordered main street. One reason for its serene, unblemished appearance is that there are no utility poles on either side of the street. Some benefactor years ago paid to have the wires and cables put underground.

The oldest house facing the street is a faded gray structure with seasoned clapboards and a superb Connecticut Valley doorway. This is the MISSION HOUSE *(Pages 84–85),* so called because it was built for John Sergeant, first missionary to the Housatonic Indians. The years have been kind to the old house, built in 1739, and today it is a superb museum of the eighteenth century way of life. Its furnishings are all of that period, making this the outstanding edifice of its kind in the Berkshires. Together with its gardens and outbuildings, it welcomes summer visitors.

The grandeur of the ISAAC ROYALL HOUSE (1732) and gardens *(Pages 86–90),* formerly surrounded by some five hundred acres of park and farmland, was the achievement of a seventeenth-century gentleman from Maine who spent many years in the West Indies amassing a fortune. He returned to New England from Antigua, his romantic and profitable career in the islands probably terminated by the uprising of the slaves, though Royall brought a dozen or more to Medford with him. His inventory at his death in 1739 records numerous "negro beds" in "the kitching", "kitching Chamber" and "garrots". It was his son, Isaac Royall, Jr. who enjoyed the beautiful estate until he went to live in England in 1775, never returning to these shores.

The land was originally the farm of Governor John Winthrop, although a later owner seems to have built the first house in about 1677. This brick structure was added to by Isaac Royall, and later by his son, to develop this beautiful early eighteenth-century mansion, now completely restored and cared for by the Royall House Association. The original seventeenth-century brickwork is still clearly visible.

Stretched along an elm-lined village street just one mile in length, Old Deerfield, Massachusetts, is one of the most rewarding places in New England. Due to the enthusiasm and the efforts of the late Henry N. Flynt and Mrs. Flynt, a dozen or more of its beautifully furnished buildings are open to the public. Antiquarian minded visitors are coming here in increasing numbers, and the hospitable village responds nobly. A whole book can be written about Deerfield houses (in fact, it has been) but we are limiting our selection to one of many, the ASHLEY HOUSE, built slightly before 1733 *(Pages 91–94).* It was bought as a new house by the Reverend Jonathan Ashley, a Yale graduate and an outspoken Tory. As a much older man during the Revolution, he was so vigorous in support of the Crown that he was locked out of his church on many a Sunday. But he was allowed to remain in the village, nonetheless, and he died in his old home in 1780. Today skilled guides welcome visitors to this restored house and others throughout the year.

Though known as the HUNTER HOUSE because of the owner, William P. Hunter, who purchased it in 1805, this house in Newport, Rhode Island, was developed to approximately its present form by Deputy Governor Jonathan Nichols, Jr., in 1748, probably by enlarging a house already at this location in about 1720 *(Pages 95–98).* Nichols was a prosperous merchant-shipper who included in his waterfront property the wharves, shops and warehouses related to an active export business. Lieutenant Governor Wanton followed him as owner in 1756, and the house was also used as headquarters for the commander of French naval forces during the Revolution. An elegant example of the earlier Georgian style, the house has been beautifully restored and furnished with fine period pieces, including some Townsend and Goddard examples. The Preservation Society of Newport County maintains and shows the Hunter House.

The fame of the JOSEPH WEBB HOUSE in Wethersfield, Connecticut *(Pages 99–100)*, came originally from the fact that General Washington and the Comte de Rochambeau met here and spent five days in May 1781, planning the Yorktown campaign. The room where Washington stayed is distinguished by a rare and delightful flock paper put on in his honor. The older part of the house, in the rear, was originally built in 1678, though it has undergone changes. The main or front section of the house was built in 1752. The house is owned by the Connecticut Society of the Colonial Dames of America.

The SILAS DEANE HOUSE, Wethersfield, Connecticut, adjoins the Webb House *(Page 100)*. The patriot Silas Deane had his mansion built in 1766 in an elegant Georgian style. The staircase is notable, and the house has good carvings done by native craftsmen. Restoration and furnishings are not yet complete, but promise to be of great beauty and authenticity. The Colonial Dames of America also own this house.

Sir William Pepperell was the only native American colonial to have been created a baronet by the Crown. He made a fortune from the sea, and a reputation for his heroic exploits at the siege of Louisburg, Nova Scotia, in 1745. His widow, Lady Mary Pepperell, built this fine Georgian mansion, the LADY PEPPERELL HOUSE at Kittery Point, Maine, in 1740 *(Pages 101–102)*. Here she is said to have lived in a certain grandeur, having a rather pretentious pride in her title. This house is a property of the SPNEA.

The great days of Salem's shipping supremacy are recalled by the RICHARD DERBY HOUSE (1761–62) sitting serenely at the head of Derby Wharf, not far from the Custom House where Nathaniel Hawthorne toiled as a clerk *(Pages 104–105)*. Richard Derby, one of the greatest of New England merchants, built this solid brick house for his son, Elias Hasket Derby, who gained even greater fame than his father. His adventures during the Revolution included fitting out privateers to prey on British shipping. At the conclusion of the war, he sent his rapid vessel *Grand Turk*, built in 1780–81, around the Cape of Good Hope, and soon this vessel was opening up trade with China. The house where this eminent man lived is now open to the public. It has been superbly restored and furnished with rare pieces. Of particular interest is the color chosen for the paneled rooms. After a great deal of research, the authentic colors have been restored, and they are delightful. This is a completely satisfactory house to visit, and color is one of the reasons. It is operated by the National Park Service.

The MOFFATT-LADD HOUSE, Portsmouth, New Hampshire, a fine three-story mansion, was built by Captain John Moffatt for his son Samuel at the time of his marriage in 1763 *(Pages 106–109)*. It is magnificently situated above the tidal river with terraced gardens at the rear. Close beside it is a small building called the counting house where the merchant-shipper carried on his business. Below were his docks and warehouses. Unfortunately, young Samuel was extravagant and not a good manager. He went bankrupt and left the country. His father, Captain John, and his sister lived in the house, and later Samuel's children and grandchildren enjoyed its spacious rooms and beautiful gardens. The grass steps, rose arbor and other plantings are traditionally parts of the early plans. The house and its surroundings are fine examples of a wealthy New England merchant's home, and authentic in every way. For this we must thank the owners and custodians, the Society of Colonial Dames of New Hampshire.

15

The JEREMIAH LEE MANSION, built in Marblehead, Massachusetts, in 1768, was the home of a wealthy merchant ship-owner who lavished what was then a fortune upon his large and beautifully appointed residence *(Pages 109–113)*. A stair hall and reception rooms of tremendous proportions, intricately carved woodwork throughout, hand painted wallpapers made to order in England, colorful Sadler and Green fireplace tiles from Liverpool, a variety of patterned iron firebacks, these are some of the original features that may be seen in the house today. His furniture has largely disappeared, though we know from the inventory of the splendid japanned cabinets, large looking glasses in carved and gilded frames, a great bed hung in crimson harrateen and another in gold silk damask. Through the years many pieces, equally handsome and suitable, have been acquired for the house by its owner, the Marblehead Historical Society, and it has become again one of the show places of the east coast. It is a Registered National Historic Landmark.

The NATHAN HALE HOMESTEAD in South Coventry, Connecticut, was named for the great patriot *(Pages 114–115)*. Curiously enough, the old farmhouse which bears his name was never inhabited by Nathan Hale himself. It was built by his family after the young hero had died. He had grown up in the earlier house on the same farm. The present house dates from 1776 and contains a tremendous amount of history within its walls in the form of family memorabilia. Deacon Richard Hale and some of his sons were justices of the Peace and held court in this house. Nathan's brother David taught school in one of the rooms. His own fowling piece hangs over the kitchen fireplace, and some of his sister Joanna's furniture and china embellishes the rooms. Surrounded by twenty acres of the original farmland, the rambling old house is truly a family homestead in the old-fashioned New England tradition. It is owned by the Antiquarian and Landmarks Society, Inc., of Connecticut.

The HATHEWAY HOUSE in Suffield, Connecticut, (which has a number of other names in its pedigree) is a delightful composite of a number of houses of different periods, added one by one by different owners *(Pages 116–119)*. The original and central section dates from about 1735–40 and contains fine woodwork typical of Connecticut at that period. In 1788 it was sold to Oliver Phelps, whose checkered career ranged from being indentured to a Suffield merchant, becoming a peddler in woodenware, serving in responsible positions for the government and making a fortune in land speculations in the Genesee Valley of New York State. Finally when he settled down once again in Suffield he added a new wing, practically another house, in 1794 to the north end of the house. He also probably added the one-story south wing as an office for himself. This appears to have been an earlier building moved from a former location. Phelps' newer north extension includes some of Asher Benjamin's designs, and contains delicate Federal woodwork and the astonishing series of French wallpapers for which the house is famous. It is owned by the Antiquarian and Landmarks Society of Connecticut, who make it open to the public.

Great political and literary figures of early New England are fairly plentiful, but there seems to be a shortage of architects. Among the latter, Charles Bulfinch and Samuel McIntire stand out with prominence. Bulfinch scattered his abilities over many parts of New England, but McIntire, with one notable exception, restricted his talents to his native town of Salem. Here he built a courthouse, the beautiful South Church on Chestnut Street and the fine assembly building, still in use for debutante parties. Hamilton Hall. But he will be remembered chiefly for his residences and for the superb wood carving which they contain. Some of his finest houses have disappeared, notably the Elias Hasket Derby House, which had an oval dining room and central stair hall in the best Bulfinch tradition, which McIntire borrowed. Its magnificence was unmatched

16

but, after the death of the owners in 1799, it never found a purchaser affluent enough to keep it up, and it was torn down in 1815.

Such a sad fate did not await McIntire's first important house, built for Jerathmeal Peirce in 1782. The PEIRCE-NICHOLS HOUSE was one of McIntire's earliest attempts, made when he was only twenty-four, and shows how carefully he studied his sources—architectural design books from England *(Pages 120–124)*. A superb Georgian mansion is the result, well planned and enriched once again by McIntire's delicate carving. In this case he also designed the urns that grace the fence posts in front of the mansion. Four furnished rooms of the Peirce-Nichols House are open to visitors, and they are truly remarkable.

The GOVERNOR JOHN LANGDON MANSION (1784), at Portsmouth, New Hampshire, is notable architecturally, but famed chiefly for its builder. John Langdon was a descendant of the first man of this name to arrive on these shores, Tobias Langdon, a Cornishman who settled here about 1650. John built this house about 1784 and, as Governor, he received many notables, including George Washington, in the large parlor or state reception room *(Pages 125–127)*. The elaborate carving of the chimney breasts of the two parlors was probably done by a member of the Dearing family, well known in the area for their work. He was possibly a son of William Dearing, ship carver of Kittery, who is said to have done the similar carving in the Chase House (1762) at Strawbery Banke. The last private owners of the house were descendants of Governor Langdon and they bequeathed it to the SPNEA.

Colonel Jonathan Hamilton, an ambitious and successful merchant in the West Indies trade, built HAMILTON HOUSE in South Berwick, Maine in 1787. It occupied the choicest site to be found on the tidewater river flowing up from Portsmouth, New Hampshire *(Pages 128–131)*. Below it were his docks and warehouses, and his vessels came and went in waters at that time busily active with traffic. One wonders at the taste and dignity displayed by this semi-educated man, though perhaps the credit belongs to his builder. As so often seen in houses somewhat remote from the big cities, the arriving Federal style is ignored, and the conservative preference for pre-Revolutionary Georgian is evident. Hamilton died in 1802 and the sea trade of Old Berwick also disappeared. A family named Goodwin owned and farmed the beautiful property for a considerable time. It was a favorite spot of Sarah Orne Jewett, who used it for the setting for her novel, THE TORY LOVER. Later she was influential in bringing the property to the compassionate attention of a wealthy Boston lady, who purchased it and used it for her summer home. As well as repairing and preserving it, she assured its future by bequeathing it with a suitable endowment to the SPNEA.

One of New England's most imposing Georgian mansions is surely the JOHN BROWN HOUSE (1786), located on the aristocratic hillside near Brown University in Providence, Rhode Island *(Pages 132–133)*. It is a large, almost square three-story edifice with a classic porch, Palladian window and other evidences of lordly design. Joseph Brown, the architect of the house, and brother of the owner, was an accomplished stylist, if he may be judged by his interiors. They are elaborate and formal, and the central stair hall is extraordinarily rich in decoration. Fashionable balls were held here in the early days, and many a commencement dinner of Brown University took place in its dining salon. The house is assured of proper care and maintenance, since it is now the home of the Rhode Island Historical Society. Arrangements may be made to visit the interior.

THE VALE in Waltham, Massachusetts, was designed and built in 1798 by Samuel McIntire for the Boston merchant, Theodore Lyman *(Pages 134–135)*. Originally of great beauty and purity of design, it

17

has been much altered and enlarged by succeeding generations of the family, which owned it until the middle of the present century. These evidences of the changing styles and of the life and taste of one family are by no means the least of the charms of this beautiful property. Many of the furnishings were Lyman possessions. The original builder was greatly interested in horticulture, and evidence of his original park and gardens remains in the broad lawns and beautiful trees, as well as one of the earliest heated greenhouses in this country. One can still see the wood-burning heating system for growing exotic fruits and plants in a cold climate. In one greenhouse there grows a Black Hamburg grapevine brought from Hampton Court in England in 1870, still healthy and producing fruit. The Vale is a property of the SPNEA, and welcomes visitors.

The JACOB WENDELL HOUSE (1789) though built in the post-Revolutionary period, remains generally Georgian in its style of an earlier day, perhaps because of local influences *(Pages 136–137)*. Woodwork and carving may have been done by craftsmen who were also responsible for some of its older neighbors.

The CHASE HOUSE, Portsmouth, New Hampshire, though built in 1762 by John Underwood of nearby Kittery, Maine, became the home of Stephen Chase, a Portsmouth merchant, later in the century and remained the home of his descendants until 1881 *(Pages 138–139)*. Here Chase entertained President George Washington during his triumphal tour in 1789. George Bigelow Chase, a wealthy philanthropist of Boston, made it a home for orphans in 1884. It was bought by Mrs. Thomas Bailey Aldrich in 1916, and she owned it until her death in 1927. It has been restored and furnished to some degree according to Stephen Chase's inventory of 1805. It is Georgian in style and the decorative wood carving of the parlor fireplace is thought to have been done by the elder William Dearing, ship carver of Kittery, Maine.

The BARRETT HOUSE at New Ipswich, New Hampshire, was built about 1800 by Charles Barrett, a pioneer industrialist originally from Concord, Massachusetts *(Pages 140–141)*. He interested himself in everything from the building of locks to the production of glass and to cotton spinning. This became the chief industry of little New Ipswich, and the continuing source of fortune to the Barrett family. The house seems to have been built for Charles Jr., at the time of his marriage, and it was owned by the family until 1948, and later bequeathed to the SPNEA.

Though the house is a three-story Federal structure, the façade retains some of the earlier Georgian feeling in a central projecting pedimented pavilion, as well as a flavor of the Greek Revival to come in the style of the front entrance. Furnishings of these several periods add interest and charm to the interior, as most of them have always been in the house and belonged to the family. The carriage house and stable wing is worth visiting, and it is said the Barrett's private coach was the first in New Ipswich.

Christopher Gore of GORE PLACE in Waltham, Massachusetts, was hardly a figure of national importance, but he loomed large in Massachusetts in the early years of the nineteenth century and before. He graduated from Harvard in the tumultuous year of 1776, and vigorously supported the patriots, though belonging to a Tory family. In the succeeding years he became a prosperous lawyer and landowner, and after the Revolution he served for eight years as *chargé d'affaires* in London on the Anglo-American claims commission established by Jay's Treaty. It was during this absence in England that plans were laid in London for Gore's country house in Waltham. While they were residing in Paris in 1801, Christopher Gore and his wife were attracted to the work of Jacques-Guillaume Legrand, a prominent Paris architect. Later Mrs. Gore sent him sketches of the house she wanted to build. This, and additional evidence points to the conclusion that the architect was French, and not British, as many had assumed. At all events it turned out to be a mansion worthy of the Governor of Massachusetts and later United States Senator, both distinctions that Christopher Gore won in later life. Gore Place (1802–1804) resembles a magnificent English estate, in spite of its French architect, and can only be compared with the great country places in Virginia, such as Carter's Grove and Westover *(Pages 142–147)*.

For a century or more Gore Place remained in private hands, but misfortune fell, as it so often does, and it became successively an automobile agency, a country club and a road house. Just in time the noble old brick mansion was rescued by a group of private citizens. Today it is secure, beautifully repaired and furnished, thanks to them. The Gore Place Society welcomes visitors and their reward is great.

The genius of Samuel McIntire is apparent once again in the finest brick house he ever designed, the imposing three-story GARDNER-PINGREE HOUSE in Salem, Massachusetts *(Pages 148–154)*. It was built in 1804 for a successful sea captain, John Gardner. Three decades later it was sold to David Pingree, and it remained in the Pingree family until it was conveyed to the Essex Institute. Today it stands in the Institute property, beautifully furnished, and is open to visitors. The best of McIntire is here, both in planning and in wood carving.

A Federal house built in 1808 and long inhabited by the Gray family and their descendants, GRAY HOUSE was later moved from its position close to the highway to another location on the same property *(Pages 155–157)*. The decoration of restrained Federal style, the high ceilings and spacious rooms are the background for eighteenth-century furniture and subtle color harmonies. All of these elements unite to form a series of interiors of great beauty.

The RUNDLET-MAY HOUSE, a delightful three-story Federal house, was built in Portsmouth, New Hampshire, by James Rundlet in 1806 and is still inhabited by his descendants *(Pages 158–159)*. The result is a home of infinite charm, filled with the original family pieces. The carving of much of the woodwork, notably the delicate frieze and the chimney breast of the parlor, may have been done by William Dearing the younger, whose work is evident in a number of Portsmouth houses. This house will soon become one of the properties of the SPNEA.

One of the most charming towns along the Coast of Maine is the ancient seaport of Wiscasset. And the most beautiful of Wiscasset's many mansions is certainly the NICKELS-SORTWELL HOUSE, a three-story Federal edifice built in 1807 *(Page 158)*. Its superb façade was designed by an unknown architect, but one obviously influenced by Bulfinch. The house was begun by Captain William Nickels, and five years were needed to complete it at a cost of $14,000, a small fortune at that time. Captain Nickels did not live long enough to enjoy his mansion very much. After his death it was run as a hostelry, Turner's Tavern, and gradually became dilapidated. Members of the Sortwell family rescued the old house, and now it stands secure under the ownership of the SPNEA.

To visit the RUGGLES HOUSE, an exquisite example of the Federal style, in this case a sort of mansion in miniature, one must go to the remote village of Columbia Falls, Maine *(Pages 160–162)*. Here in about 1817 the local lumber king, Thomas Ruggles, had his house built in what was the most up-to-date style and with such sophisticated features as a divided free-standing staircase and elaborately carved though restrained interior woodwork. The reason for this rather unexpected appearance lies, no doubt, in Ruggles' own success and prominence, the fact that he came from southern Massachusetts, and that he imported an architect of fine reputation, Aaron Simmons Sherman from Marshfield, Massachusetts. The timely rescue of this little

19

jewel, its restoration and furnishings should be credited to the efforts of Miss Mary Ruggles Chandler, last of the family (and incidentally the first registered woman pharmacist in Maine), and the Ruggles Historical Society. Here many Ruggles family pieces have been restored to their proper place under this roof. This is a gentleman's house of the Federal period, though its small scale and naïveté of expression, both inside and out, relate the house to its background in a small Maine village.

The DESHON-ALLYN HOUSE stands in the grounds of the Lyman-Allyn Museum in New London, Connecticut, a park-like area which was originally part of a forty-four acre property belonging to the Bolles family *(Pages 163–165)*. They sold it to Daniel Deshon in 1802. In 1829 this granite house was built for his son. Though the Greek Revival was coming into fashion, this house shows the conservatism of New England taste in clinging to many features of the foregoing Federal style. It has been noted that the influence of the architect, Asher Benjamin, is apparent in many of its details. Interestingly furnished with pieces of the late Federal and Empire styles, many of which belonged to the Deshons and the later owners, the Allyns, the house is owned and maintained by the Lyman-Allyn Museum.

The VASSALL-CRAIGIE-LONGFELLOW HOUSE was built in 1759 in Cambridge, Massachusetts, by Major John Vassall, a young Tory, and used by General Washington as his headquarters in 1775. It was purchased and enlarged by Andrew Craigie in 1793, but it is really as the home of the beloved poet Henry Wadsworth Longfellow, that this old house is known and visited *(Pages 166–169)*. He lived here in lodgings as a young professor of Modern Languages at Harvard in 1837, and became owner of the house after his marriage to Miss Frances Appleton of Boston, remaining here until his death in 1882. In spite of pre-Revolutionary bevelled panels, fine spiralled balusters and a great Georgian chimney of imposing classic style, this was and is Longfellow's house; Victorian and cluttered, homelike and cozy, it is furnished as he left it. From his pens in the study to the portrait of his three little daughters of "The Children's Hour", this is the Longfellow House.

A Victorian city house built in Boston, Massachusetts just before the Civil War (1859), the GIBSON HOUSE is of interest as a specimen of this period, intact in every way *(Page 170)*. It has been kept exactly as the family left it, with practically all of its original furnishings. This is of great value and interest to students of this period. It is now a Boston museum, and can be visited.

Though built in 1811 by James Hazeltine, the GOVERNOR GOODWIN MANSION, in Portsmouth, New Hampshire, has been known chiefly as the home of Ichabod Goodwin, who acquired it in 1832 *(Pages 171–173)*. As a young man he had gone to sea, then became a merchant, prosperous business man and manufacturer. He served in the State Legislature and became Governor of New Hampshire in 1859. His daughter married George Dewey, later the Admiral famous for his victory at Manila Bay. The house is furnished mainly in the Empire and Victorian styles of Goodwin's period and contains some pieces owned by or connected with his family. Some of the carving is said to have been done by the younger William Dearing whose work appears in a number of Portsmouth buildings.

KINGSCOTE was built in 1842 in Newport, Rhode Island by architect Richard Upjohn for Noble Jones and sold in 1864 to William H. King who gave it its name *(Pages 174–175)*. An early example of the Gothic asymmetrical style, it is informal and picturesque with lacy trim on steep pitched gables, wide overhanging eaves and crennelated bays. Inside, the dark woodwork of the hall includes an arcade with pointed arches. The rooms contain a varied and fine collection of Chinese objects gathered by Mr. King during his many years in trade with the Orient.

20

There is a cluster of five or six villages using the name of Woodstock—East, West, North, South and Center, all in the far northeast corner of Connecticut. They all have rural charm, but our favorite is plain Woodstock without any prefix. Built around a very wide village green, its stately white houses and town buildings reflect reposeful rural charm. But one of these houses isn't white; it's pink, with dark red trim and unmistakable Gothic lines. This is ROSELAND COTTAGE, built in 1846, and there is nothing quite like it in America *(Pages 176–177)*. Its architect, Joseph C. Wells, had individual ideas about a house. Rural Gothic, he maintained "speaks of quiet domestic feeling and the family circle. A Gothic house should have secluded shadowy corners, nooks where one would love to linger, cosy rooms where fireside joys are invited to dwell." The original owner of Roseland Cottage, Henry Chandler Bowen, was a native of Woodstock though a wealthy Brooklyn newspaper publisher, and this was his summer home. He was a friend of celebrities, and four presidents—Hayes, Harrison, Cleveland and McKinley—were all overnight guests at Roseland Cottage. Many guests enjoyed his private bowling alley built in a barn behind the house, including Ulysses S. Grant, who made a ten strike. In addition to presidents, such notables as Harriett Beecher Stowe, Oliver Wendell Holmes and Julia Ward Howe were guests here.

VICTORIA MANSION in Portland, Maine, owes its style and its name to the owner's tremendous admiration for England's Queen and her consort, Prince Albert the builder. Those who have visited Osborne House on the Isle of Wight, perhaps Queen Victoria's favorite residence, and designed by Prince Albert, will see at once the relationship in exterior style. Ruggles Sylvester Morse, a son of Maine who had later amassed a fortune in New Orleans and then returned to Portland, engaged a famous architect of the day, Henry Austin, to design his house and lavished half a million dollars upon its creation *(Pages 178–180)*. It was built between 1859 and 1863. The superlative quality of materials and workmanship used in the interior decoration and furnishings cannot be ignored. Victoria Mansion is truly a monument to the period, which the Queen herself would have loved.

The CHARLESTON HOUSE is placed last in our collection because it was actually constructed in 1923 *(Pages 181–184)*. Thus, it follows our attempt to place these New England rooms approximately in sequence according to date, as nearly as certain physical requirements of book-making allow. Of course the main beauty of the house, apart from its furnishings, is the woodwork from Charleston, South Carolina, which dates from about 1800. Recognition is due to the builder, who had the taste and the foresight to rescue at least a part of a fine structure doomed to destruction by the march of "progress"—in this case a railroad.

This brings to a close our selection of fifty-six New England houses with interesting interiors, built between 1639 and the twentieth century. They have been chosen from a wide field, and many more could be added to the list, if the narrow confines of an illustrated book permitted.

We would like to terminate these paragraphs with a warm note of thanks to the generous people who have helped us, and permitted us to invade their premises with lights, cameras and notebooks. We are grateful to many local historical societies, to larger organizations we have already mentioned, as well as to many private individuals. All have made notable contributions in preserving our New England heritage, and they deserve a rising vote of thanks.

SAMUEL CHAMBERLAIN
NARCISSA G. CHAMBERLAIN

THE NEW ENGLAND ROOMS

The symbol of seventeenth-century New England is expressed in this Connecticut kitchen. Built of native stone, the broad fireplace is spanned by a massive oak lintel that has defied the centuries. A brick oven is built into one side, while the hearth is made up of giant flat stones. Sturdy ladder-back chairs stand sentinel by the fireplace, where the equipment to create a fine New England meal is ready at hand.

Built in 1639, the HENRY WHITFIELD HOUSE has the distinction of being the oldest stone dwelling in New England. Standing in the open fields on the southern outskirts of Guilford, Connecticut, it served the multiple purpose of church, meeting house and fort, as well as the residence of the town's first minister and his family. On the ground floor is the great hall, thirty-three feet long with a fireplace at each end. A hinged partition of feathered boards is fastened to the ceiling, to be lowered at will to form two smaller rooms, and raised at meeting time to accommodate a gathering of people. The house was completely restored in 1937, and is now a state historical museum.

The North Chamber (left) has been furnished as it might have looked when the minister's wife lived in it. The massive fireplace is built into the stone end of the house.

26

The first crude ironworks in the Colonies was built in Saugus, Massachusetts, in 1642. In connection with this early enterprise, Thomas Dexter erected the old IRONMASTER'S HOUSE in 1643. This noble seventeenth-century dwelling went through its share of misfortunes before being restored in 1915 by Wallace Nutting. He contributed many of the early pieces of furniture that now embellish the house. The Saugus Ironworks is now under the supervision of the Department of the Interior, and welcomes visitors.

An upper bedroom of the Ironmaster's House is neat and cheerful, if a trifle sparse. At this early period the only windows consisted of small diamond-shaped panes, imported from England, and set in iron frames with lead. Animal skins were the only rugs.

In the kitchen of the Ironmaster's House *(opposite above)* is a wide fireplace spanned by a lengthy wooden lintel. Drying herbs hang from a pole, and a musket reposes, ready for use, on the lintel.

A bedroom shows the sturdy construction of the beamed ceiling, upheld by a chamfered summer beam and gunstock corner posts *(opposite below)*. The folding bed can be turned up under the shallow canopy. Adjoining it stands a child's cradle.

Wood-burning fireplaces offered the only means of heating these chilly rooms. Above the lintel often appeared a few shelves to house the family's small collection of books *(right)*.

The Great Hall of the Ironmaster's House reveals the immense ceiling beams of oak, some of them two feet square. The wide brick fireplace is fitted with a mechanical spit, iron pots, hooks, cranes and other essentials for cooking. An ancient carved document box rests on the table rug in the foreground, near which is placed a wainscot chair.

The ancient town of Ipswich, Massachusetts, is celebrated for its many seventeenth-century houses, one of the oldest of which is the WHIPPLE HOUSE, built about 1640 by John Fawn *(opposite above)*. It was later acquired by the Whipple family, who made several additions. The house has been restored and furnished by the Ipswich Historical Society, and is open to visitors during the warmer months. Early pine shadow molding sheathing appears here.

The brick fireplace of the Whipple House *(opposite below)*, is framed with restored wide moldings and sheathing. Over it hangs an overmantel painted panel depicting the mouth of the Ipswich River before the Revolution. A child's wainscot chair, a late seventeenth-century Ipswich chest, and a carved Ipswich document box (probably by Dennis) are at the left.

A glimpse of the upper hall of the Ironmaster's House *(left)* shows the fine old stairway with newel posts, turned balusters, and a small pendant.

The upper chamber or parlor of the Whipple House has a great deal of style, with a reproduction of a three-part leaded window, a local Chippendale writing desk and a tall-case clock by Silas Hadley of Plymouth, Connecticut (early nineteenth century). A central gate-legged table is noteworthy as are two Queen Anne armchairs with turned and blocked forelegs and Spanish feet.

A Whipple House bed chamber is fitted with a Sheraton field bed with a netted canopy. The later date of such pieces in the house (c. 1800) is justified by the fact that the Whipple family descendants lived here until 1833.

ANTIQUARIAN HOUSE, in Concord, Massachusetts, is one of the finest museums of early period rooms in New England. Built in 1930, it assembles a series of historic rooms ranging from the seventeenth century, here illustrated, to an Empire room dating from about 1825. In addition, there is a duplicate of Ralph Waldo Emerson's study with all the author's books and furnishings, and a small, slant-ceilinged room duplicating the hut at Walden Pond where Henry Thoreau lived and wrote. The building is owned by the Concord Antiquarian Society, and is open to visitors from early spring to late autumn.

A seventeenth-century wing of Antiquarian House illustrates the Concord way of life around 1690–1700 when a certain degree of comfort had asserted itself. In this typical early New England "hall" the furnishings are in the best English tradition. A gate-leg table, Carolean chairs with carved crests and stretchers, and chests with shallow carving show the early Colonial taste.

Framed in ancient vertical sheathing, the deep fireplace dominates the seventeenth-century wing *(opposite above)*. It is made of large uneven bricks and is surrounded by a restrained molding. From the lugpole hangs a hefty iron cauldron, a standby in feeding the pioneer family. Standing next to the fireplace is a stern wooden settle with a high back to cut off drafts of cold air. A low primitive rocking chair occupies the foreground.

Most of the walls in this room *(opposite below)* are simply plastered, providing a good foil for the fine old Carver chairs, the press cupboard, geometrically paneled chest and early ornaments.

One of the noteworthy pieces in this room is an important American oak press cupboard *(left)*. It was used to store provisions.

34

Another fireplace has a brick oven with wooden door, and a wooden peel to remove the loaves of bread when done. Notable are the wainscot and Carver chairs and a small trestle table covered with a carpet in the seventeenth-century fashion.

The pine-ceilinged room in the Antiquarian House is one of the very few that have survived in this country. It was found in Hampton, New Hampshire, and installed here with only the windows as reproductions. A cheerful if primitive corner cupboard gives a decorative touch to this severe little room.

The TRISTRAM COFFIN HOUSE in Old Newbury, Massachusetts, began as a small building, now an ell, built in 1651. The ancient kitchen is almost unchanged after more than three centuries. The venerable dresser is lined with old pewter, and the fireplace is equipped with trammels, iron pots and a brick oven to care for the family appetite. The paneled wall with three adjoining cupboards is most unusual. The round family table is surrounded by much later "birdcage" Windsor chairs with bamboo turnings. The Tristram Coffins produced ten children and many distinguished descendants.

HEMPSTED HOUSE, the oldest in New London, Connecticut, was built by Joshua Hempsted in 1678 and enlarged by his grandson fifty years later. Still located on its original wooded plot of land, it is now owned and maintained by the Antiquarian and Landmarks Society, Inc. of Connecticut. Many original Hempsted pieces still furnish the primitive rooms. On the eighteenth-century side of the house is the kitchen, one wall of which is wide whitewashed brick. The fireplace opening is spanned by a solid stone lintel. Pewter, crockery and wooden plates are aligned on the shelves. The primitive hutch table is surrounded by ladder-back chairs, one for the baby of the family.

The seventeenth-century hall preserves the Hempsted bed that always occupied this corner *(opposite above)*. Its hangings are deep green. In the foreground is an oval gate-leg table used for dining. Carver chairs are plentiful here. The beamed ceiling has been painted white, adding a little light to the room.

Joshua Hempsted's chamber is rather austere, its very plain fireplace flanked by a door and a primitive cupboard *(opposite below)*. The drop-leaf Queen Anne table has style, as do the early chairs.

An early fireplace *(right)* is made up of wide blocks of carved stone, spanned by a sturdy lintel of wood. Framing the end of the room is a heavy chamfered summer beam.

The STANLEY-WHITMAN HOUSE in Farmington, Connecticut, a fine early dwelling with a frontal overhang and a central stone chimney, dates from about 1660. It was restored in 1934 and now serves as a museum of Connecticut antiquity. One outstanding room has an extraordinary Georgian mantel, a later addition put over an enormous early fireplace. It has few if any rivals of this type in New England.

Built about 1692 in the ancient town of Wethersfield, Connecticut, the BUTTOLPH-WILLIAMS HOUSE has been restored in recent years and furnished with appropriate pieces of the period. The "Greate Hall" chamber, *(two views opposite)* is a room of great dignity, dominated by a bed with voluminous hangings and a valance of flame-stitch embroidery. At the left is a seventeenth-century New England chest.
Bannister-back New England chairs with richly carved crests lend dignity to the setting. A fine bolection molding frames the fireplace opening.

Another kitchen in the Hempsted House in New London *(left)* has a fireplace built of massive field stone. Drying herbs hang from the original wooden herb pole. In the foreground is a rare and very substantial seventeenth-century cradle.

The WHITE-ELLERY HOUSE, one of the most ancient dwellings in Gloucester, Massachusetts, stood squarely in the path of the roadbuilders as they sought to construct a traffic circle on the outskirts of the town a few decades ago. Public-spirited citizens rescued the old salt-box house which dated from 1703 and had been a parsonage as well as the town tavern. It was moved in 1947 to a suitable site nearby, furnished with a wealth of antiques and opened as a museum house.

"The Greate Hall" or parlor of the Buttolph-Williams House *(opposite above)* has simple dignity, with bannister-back chairs grouped around a gate-leg table. On the fireplace shelf are delft plates of the early period, and a brass lantern clock keeps time on the wall.

"The Kitchin Chamber" of the same house is embellished with slat-back armchairs and an ample gate-leg table. This is one of the museum houses owned and maintained by the Antiquarian and Landmarks Society, Inc. of Connecticut.

Much of the furniture and collections of household objects in the White-Ellery House *(right)* were gathered by the late Mr. and Mrs. Albert H. Atkins, and were formerly in the old Haskell House, built before 1652, in West Gloucester, Massachusetts.

43

The kitchen of the White-Ellery House is primitive but well equipped, particularly with pewter. The structural feature of commanding interest is the corner post, braced by two angular supports, a favorite device of early English builders. An attempt at decoration is visible on the wide beam supporting the ceiling.

The brick fireplace of this kitchen with two commodious ovens, serves as a background to display part of the Atkins collection of iron porringers, skewers, triform hooks, toasters, broilers, forks and tongs.

One of the most remarkable house museums in America is BEAUPORT, the assemblage of a score or more of period rooms under one roof at Eastern Point, in Gloucester, Massachusetts. This page is limited to the pine kitchen, known as the Pembroke Room, a superb study of early Americana assembled by the former owner, Henry Sleeper. An inveterate collector and a skilled decorator, Mr. Sleeper created a remarkable mansion of many moods. It is open to the public during the summer months, and shouldn't be missed.

The PARSON CAPEN HOUSE in Topsfield, Massachusetts, was built by the Reverend Joseph Capen in 1683, the village preacher who served there for forty years. The house is still in good condition, and is considered one of the finest examples of Elizabethan architecture in America. The parlor was used for retirement and the entertainment of special guests. Its beamed ceiling has been painted white, adding cheer to the room. Around the gate-leg table are grouped three chairs, and the one on the right is Parson Capen's own, his name being carved on the crest. The wide fireplace is for heating purposes only.

The hall of the Parson Capen House *(opposite above)*, which served as a living room, dining room and kitchen combined, is commodious and unadorned. The stern wooden stools and solid tables are not designed for comfort.

The kitchen fireplace *(opposite below)* is utilitarian in every way, with ample kettles and a brick oven. It is spanned by a huge whitewashed wooden lintel.

The hallway *(right)* is severe and unpainted, the turned balusters of the stair rail being the only decorative feature. The sturdy oak newel post is the original, unchanged since 1683.

47

48

The ABRAHAM BROWNE, JR. HOUSE in Watertown, Massachusetts, has been restored thanks to the Society for the Preservation of New England Antiquities. It was built around 1690, and is notable for its seventeenth-century hall, surely one of the most remarkable period rooms in New England. The only known original three-part window frame, built to hold diamond-shaped panes imported from England, was found in this house during the restoration. The room *(above)* is completely equipped for family life, including a well-protected bed. An early New England cupboard, bedecked with pewter, stands against the far wall.

An unusually wide brick fireplace *(opposite above)* is spanned by a tremendous hand-hewn oak lintel. A fine early carved wainscot bench stands on the foreground. Both horizontal and vertical sheathing are visible in the lower picture, which shows a noble Carver chair.

A sturdy trestle table, setting for the family meals, is covered with an intricate "Turkey carpet". A reproduction of the three-piece window frame lets in light from the garden.

TIME STONE FARM in eastern Massachusetts, dates from 1702 and preserves the atmosphere of that early period with entire fidelity. It began as one large room with a stone chimney and eventually grew to eleven rooms, each with its own fireplace. Above is one of the eleven, made of field stone, and equipped with a brass clock jack to turn the spit. The table is set with a loaf of bread, a chunk of cheese, and a jug of wine, surely the essentials of happiness.

The Great Room *(opposite above),* earliest part of the house, is the setting for a long trestle table, set with heavy pottery plates. Wooden benches and stools accommodate the dinner guests with no needless show of comfort. Bear skins served as rugs in those days.

A bedroom fireplace *(opposite below)* maintains a ready musket on the fireplace lintel. Three heavily turned, early armchairs, each different, cluster around a small tavern table.

A corner of the old kitchen *(right)* shows a primitive cupboard loaded with a collection of early pottery.

51

A front bedroom on the second floor of Time Stone Farm was decorated with stencil wall ornamentation in green and russet tones. A part of this is restoration.

Another fireplace *(opposite above)* is furnished with a crane and a separate oven. It is brightened by pewter and old paintings.

This may have been the fireplace in the corner *(opposite below)* chosen by Uncle Nathan Goodale, who lived and cooked apart from the large Goodale family.

This bedroom *(left)* is in the lean-to added about 1740. The bedstead has an arched tester hung with old chintz. The bed coverlet is an appliqué quilt with floral motifs.

The OGDEN HOUSE is a Connecticut farmhouse with all the indications of its early origin. Exposed ceiling beams and corner posts, the immense central stone chimney and broad hearths, wide floor boards and multi-paned windows all form a background for a superb collection of early furniture and household utensils. The living room contains a display of redware, largely from Connecticut. Other ornaments include the charming tin chandelier and a wooden bird decoy.

The original kitchen of the Ogden House, now a study, contains a group of bannister chairs of various designs. The celestial and terrestrial globes are by James Wilson, first American globe maker. The portraits of Sarah and Jesse Stedman, by Asahel Powers, dominate the wall area.

In the dining room *(right)* a decorated chest retains its painted designs in a condition of great clarity. The reverse-bannister side chairs are two of a set of six with their original black paint. The William Jennys portrait of Nathaniel Lamsan is one of the finest in the house.

The paneling of the north chamber of the Ogden House is unpainted, as well as being simpler in finish than the other rooms. The panels have no quarter round molding next to the bevel, which indicates a room of lesser importance. The portrait is a pastel by Micah Williams.

The dining room of the Ogden House *(opposite above)* is painted a soft grey-green, reproducing the original tone. The recessed chimney breast has a strong bolection molding framing the opening. The Queen Anne Spanish-foot chairs retain their original black paint.

Another member of the Stedman family, also by Powers, hangs on the study wall gazing into what was originally the kitchen fireplace *(opposite below)*.

All of the furniture in the north chamber *(right)* retains its old painted finish, including a rare Connecticut chest at the foot of the pencil-post bed.

The south chamber walls of the Ogden House are red-stained sheathing. The crane-top folding bed, once owned by Thomas Danforth, the pewterer, is hung with blue and white furniture check and an indigo linsey-woolsey coverlet.

The Connecticut high chest in the south chamber *(left)* is cherry, and carries some of a collection of hat boxes all covered with blue papers of various patterns.

The BUBIER MANSION on the shore north of Boston, dates from about 1700–1720, and inclines to spare and simple interior finish, functional and well proportioned. A fine example of the central chimney type, the house contains six fireplaces and originally had two owners who apparently shared the chimney stack. At an early date one owner bought out the other and later put a gambrel roof over the whole house, covering what had been the pent with a small second story room. The original kitchen has become a library, paneled with pine sheathing set in tongue and groove fashion. The old fireplace is surrounded by a few cooking utensils and English horse brasses. A pair of early ladder-back armchairs flank the hearth.

Bookshelves framed with pine boards of a deep mellow tone that comes from age alone add warm color to the room. A Spanish choir stool stands beside a French country Empire chair. The long eighteenth-century table, probably of chestnut, may once have graced a French country kitchen.

59

The BUBIER MANSION is north of Boston. The living room contains a fine Louis XIV provincial commode with characteristic ornate brasses. Above it hangs a Louis XVI looking-glass, and flanking it are two gilded, English Regency side chairs. Two French armchairs, one Louis XVI on the left and the other Louis XV, occupy the foreground. On the floor are several unusual American oval rugs of the smallest possible braiding, with colorful hooked centers.

The sunny, cheerful dining room *(opposite above)* contains both French and American pieces. A Louis XVI chest of drawers with marble top serves as a sideboard. Behind it hangs a Jacquard wool coverlet, woven in tones of deep blue, rust and natural beige. The mahogany dining table is a Hepplewhite drop-leaf one with inlays of thistle and vine leaves.

The dining-room fireplace is slightly recessed *(opposite below)* and the panel above is formed by a single wide board. The trim of this room is an Indian red used in early houses. On the hearth rests a pair of early eighteenth-century candle stands. A two-drawer Louis XVI chest stands to the right, and over it hangs a rare, very small French *panetière*.

A bedroom is furnished with a cherry four-post bed from the early nineteenth century, covered with a quilt made in cross-and-crown pattern (also called goose tracks and bear's paws). The walnut William and Mary dressing table is American, and the dressing glass English Queen Anne.

61

The RICHARD WEBB HOUSE was built about 1700. It has been moved from a neighboring city and reconstructed, piece by piece, on a site in the open country not far away. There its new owners restored the old salt-box and furnished it with antique pieces that they had collected. The dining room *(above)* has early pine paneling and exposed ceiling beams. The pewter in the cupboard is by Connecticut craftsmen. The fringed cloth covers the dining table when not in use, as in the early days.

The parlor of the Webb House *(opposite above)* is finished in typical Connecticut paneling, which includes a superb corner cupboard. The trumpet-leg William and Mary high chest and the Queen Anne chairs are of the period.

The fireplace paneling *(opposite below)* with rudimentary pilasters is typical of Connecticut. The easy chair is covered with crewelwork of eighteenth-century design, made by the owner.

The late seventeenth-century pine stretcher dining table *(right)* is set with Lambeth delft plates, early pewter mugs, forks and spoons, and illuminated by a small brass chandelier of the period.

The old kitchen, now the living room of the Webb House, has a paneled overmantel. The chimney is typical of Connecticut stone construction. Bannister-back chairs, gate-leg tables and early utensils and ornaments complete the picture.

Dull yellow-green paneling, a quaint red wing chair perhaps constructed on an early base, a fine New England bannister-back chair and a folding bed of the late eighteenth century furnish a beautiful bedroom of the Webb House (opposite above).

A chamfered summer beam and gunstock corner posts uphold the unplastered ceiling of another bedroom (opposite below). An early maple chest of drawers, a turned Carver chair, a crane-top folding bed, and a turned, convertible table-chair are authentic period furnishings.

A bannister-back armchair and a slat-back rocker flank a small tavern table which holds a game of checkers. Wavy slats may indicate a French Canadian origin.

The PARSON BARNARD HOUSE in North Andover, Massachusetts, was long considered the seventeenth-century home of Anne Bradstreet, early American poetess. Recent research has shown that it was built about 1718 by the Reverend Thomas Barnard, the local pastor. The upper west chamber is sheathed with exceptionally wide pine boards, stained brown. The geometrically paneled oak chest is painted red and black and dates from about 1700. The writing box upon it is of the same period. Open upon the table rug is a Bible Concordance containing the minister's signature and dated 1702.

This view of the chamber called Thomas's room *(right)* shows the spare simple style of furnishings suitable to such an early room. A folding bed of red-painted birch, an oak Carver chair of the late seventeenth century and a tape loom are visible, as well as an English document box on the floor below the window.

The lower east parlor is known as the Reverend Mr. Symmes room. He came here in 1757 and lived here as minister until 1807. The furnishings are in keeping with his later times and include a tall-case clock by Simon Willard, a walnut fall-front desk and a corner commode chair. The rug is an antique Soumac from Kashmir.

66

The paneling of the fireplace wall of the east parlor was probably installed in this room after the Reverend Mr. Symmes arrived with his new bride from Boston in 1757. Above the even later mantel hangs a series of six early color prints representing the story of the Prodigal Son. Most of the furniture is Queen Anne in style.

The WARNER HOUSE (1716) in Portsmouth, New Hampshire, is one of the finest urban brick houses of the first quarter of the eighteenth century. The dining room *(above)* is richly paneled. Its walls are embellished with an early example of painted foliate decoration. The brass chandelier is either English or Dutch, while the oak gate-leg table is probably English, and so is the Chippendale chair. The china is mostly China Trade porcelain.

The upper east chamber of the Parson Barnard House *(opposite above)* is known as John Barnard's room. The trim and inside shutters are painted a muted green-blue. The pencil-post bed is dressed with crewelwork in an eighteenth-century pattern. The painted William and Mary chest-on-frame was found in Essex County. An American gate-leg table of about 1710 is set with pewter and table wares of the period.

The maple desk in the same room *(opposite below)* descended in the Abbot family in Andover. The fireplace wall is the unchanged original, the panels being formed by applied moldings. Those on the left open to disclose a cupboard with shelves grooved to hold plates.

Another view of the Warner House dining room *(right)* shows a fine English sideboard. The portraits of Mr. and Mrs. Jonathan Warner are by Joseph Blackburn.

In a graceful bedroom of the Warner House, an ancient seventeenth-century carved chest sits at the foot of the canopied bed. The Chippendale mirror hangs over a fine New England chest of drawers (*c.* 1800).

The parlor of the Warner House *(opposite above)* is finely paneled. Its most conspicuous ornament is a Joseph Blackburn portrait of Miss Polly Warner at the age of twelve. The room is large, almost twenty feet square, with an eleven-foot ceiling. The Philadelphia desk in the corner contains China Trade porcelain destined for the French market. The crystal chandelier is supposed to have shone on Lafayette when he visited Portsmouth in 1825.

The parlor fireplace *(opposite below)* is built across the corner of the room instead of being set in a wall. It is faced with ancient Dutch tiles. Under Miss Polly's portrait is a Portsmouth Chippendale silver table.

The central stair hall of the Warner House *(right)* is adorned with extraordinary murals depicting the Indian sachems taken to England by Peter Schuyler in 1710.

The great room above the parlor of the Warner House has similar ample proportions. This was called the Council Chamber when Benning Wentworth, governor of the province, occupied the house in the 1750's. The dignified personage in the Blackburn portrait is Sarah Macpheadris, the governor's sister. The four chairs in the foreground were made in Portsmouth in 1728.

In the corner of the Council Chamber is a desk with a serpentine front, above which hangs a portrait of Nathaniel Warner, also by Blackburn.

On the second floor of the house is the children's room, well equipped with toys and undersized furniture.

A canopied bed is fitted with an American crewelwork coverlet.

An early walnut veneered cabinet is also open for inspection.

Two handsome rooms represent the early eighteenth century in the Antiquarian House in Concord, Massachusetts. The Green Room *(above)* shows paneling assembled with pilasters in an informal manner, and painted a soft green. The bannister-back chairs were owned by early settlers of the town. Rare silver pieces are displayed in a cupboard. The Queen Anne Room *(below)* shows old pine paneling which has never been painted. A fine New England easy chair, the tea table and the side chairs all show the New England version of the Queen Anne style. The armchair is earlier.

The sunny kitchen of the CROWNINSHIELD-BENTLEY HOUSE in Salem, Massachusetts, with lead grey paint and a black dado, is a worthy setting for a collection of kitchen implements which follows a 1761 Crowninshield inventory.

The sunny early parlor *(above)* was furnished according to John Crowninshield's inventory. A seventeenth-century Essex County chest stands between the windows.

The later parlor, renovated in 1794 but in the style of about 1770, contains Chippendale and Queen Anne furniture, mostly of local origin. The graceful window hangings were designed after ones depicted in a Ralph Earl portrait of the period.

76

The restoration of the CROWNINSHIELD-BENTLEY HOUSE in Salem, Massachusetts, is one of the good deeds done by the Essex Institute in recent years. The old house on Essex Street was rescued before the wreckers could level it. It was moved to the grounds of the Essex Institute, restored with care, and furnished with appropriate pieces, mainly of the region, in memory of the late Louise du Pont Crowninshield. Built by John Crowninshield in 1727, the house is celebrated as the residence of William Bentley, noted clergyman, diarist and gossip. The house represents the early period of the builder's time as well as middle and late eighteenth-century changes and additions. A rear bedroom of this house *(above)* reveals a well-balanced arrangement of a Salem Sheraton chest of drawers, a Federal mirror, and a pair of old English prints.

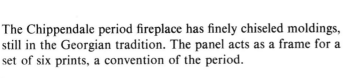
The Chippendale period fireplace has finely chiseled moldings, still in the Georgian tradition. The panel acts as a frame for a set of six prints, a convention of the period.

77

A Federal bedroom in the Crowninshield-Bentley House *(above)* is dominated by a fine Sheraton canopied bed. A gentleman's washstand with a brass basin stands before the left window.

The Reverend Dr. Bentley's room located in the early side of this house, where he lived for so many years, *(opposite above)* is comfortable and well appointed. The fireplace moldings are painted in two tones, following similar colors derived from uncovering the early paint. In the panel hangs a watercolor of the blockade of Boston Bay in 1768, by Christian Remick. Books, a tea caddy and one chair in the room are Dr. Bentley's. There are facilities for afternoon tea.

A fine walnut Queen Anne high chest and a dressing table, both Essex County pieces, furnish a bedroom of the middle period of the house *(opposite below)*. The window curtains were designed after those in an old painting.

The original kitchen *(left)* is furnished with a fireplace capable of handling any type of dish with the aid of a weighted spit, pots, skewers, trivets, toaster, skimmer and a large wooden peel for handling loaves of bread.

A great deal of history grew up around the old hip-roofed house on the outskirts of Middletown, Rhode Island. It still stands serene behind its stone wall, and bears the proud name of WHITEHALL. It was named by its early owner, the Very Reverend George Berkeley, Dean of Londonderry in Ireland, and a famed philosopher. His stay in the Colonies was brief, and he returned in 1731 to England, giving his library of 880 volumes to Yale University. He also gave Whitehall to Yale, and the rent derived from it provided a scholarship known as "The Dean's Bounty." In later years Whitehall became a public house run by a Mr. Anthony, whose daughter became the mother of Gilbert Stuart, the great American portraitist. The old building is now maintained as an historical shrine by the Colonial Dames of America, and is open to the public in summer. The parlor seems rather severe, and is fitted with a Windsor chair with a Chippendale splat and a restrained paneled early bench that looks none too comfortable.

The walls of Whitehall are white plaster, and the furniture is simple. The chair in front of the window is a *prie-dieu,* or prayer chair.

The Green Room of Whitehall is the most ambitious room in the old house. Its fireplace is framed by a bolection molding above which is a panel of unusual width. A delicate bannister-back chair and an early corner chair stand before it.

The sunny parlor in Whitehall has a fireplace faced with early delft tiles and an ancient seventeenth-century New England chest. Every attempt has been made to furnish the house as it would have been in the Dean's time.

The SHORT HOUSE, built about 1733, is an early brick-end house on the High Road in Old Newbury, Massachusetts. Inside are two finely paneled eighteenth-century rooms, both unpainted. The parlor *(above)* has a pilastered fireplace and a well-designed arched cupboard for china. Carved William and Mary chairs stand around the drop-leaf Queen Anne table.

The PUTNAM COTTAGE in Greenwich, Connecticut, *(opposite)* was built along the old Post Road in 1731. Originally it was Knapp's Tavern. According to local history, General Israel Putnam was staying at this tavern when it was attacked by the British in February 1779. The General adroitly escaped from the Red Coats by plunging down the hill over a steep incline with his horse. Recent restorations in the house have exposed the full extent of the huge fieldstone fireplace. It is spanned by a massive hand-hewn lintel and has a large oven that extends into another fireplace in the adjoining room. This room has also been restored recently, and the fireplace opening has been framed in paneling. Putnam Cottage is owned by the Daughters of the American Revolution, and is open to the public.

The bedroom fireplace of the Short House *(left)* is delicate and refined, with good pilasters and panels, all in unpainted wood.

The MISSION HOUSE in Stockbridge, Massachusetts, in the Berkshires, was built in 1739 for John Sergeant, the young tutor at Yale College who gave up his position to become the first missionary to the Housatonic Indians. He was ordained in Deerfield before a distinguished audience including the Governor, the Council, and many Indians. The house has been well preserved, and all of its furnishings are over two centuries old. It was restored in recent years by Miss Mabel Choate, and is now owned by a local association, and is open to visitors during the warmer months of the year. The dining room presents an orderly picture of New England life with a large pine dresser stocked with pewter, a corner livery cupboard and a trestle table surrounded by country Chippendale chairs.

All of the furniture in this room *(left)* is said to date before 1749, and some of it belonged to John Sergeant himself. It includes a Queen Anne high chest, several early "courting" mirrors or looking-glasses, a Carver chair, and a desk-on-frame.

This paneled room of the Mission House is informal and unsymmetrical. A musket waits ready over the mantel, which is bedecked with a succession of kitchen implements.

A Queen Anne easy chair, beautifully finished with crewelwork, stands before the paneled and pilastered fireplace. A rachet candleholder is near the grate.

One of the most fascinating houses in Massachusetts, both historically and architecturally, is the ISAAC ROYALL HOUSE, begun as a brick farmhouse in the seventeenth century, and finished as a three-storied mansion in 1732. The dining room is built against the brick wall of the Governor John Winthrop farmhouse, and its table is American Queen Anne of about 1740. The Chippendale chairs were made in the Boston area and the paneling is painted to resemble cedar graining.

The magnificent woodwork of the west parlor *(opposite above)* is painted a pale blue-green. The delft fireplace tiles are puce, or plum color, and in rarely intact condition. A paler shade of this color is used in damask hangings and chair seats.

The west parlor provides a glimpse into the east parlor of the Isaac Royall House *(opposite below)*. An English nineteenth-century tall-case clock by Strandring of Bolton, and a beechwood Queen Anne English daybed with period flame-stitch upholstery are at the left.

In the dining room *(left)* a mahogany looking-glass with gilded carving, broken arch pediment and a phoenix bird, hangs between the windows.

A chamber in the Isaac Royall House is named in honor of the D.A.R. chapter that at one time rented the house for its meetings, and was really responsible for starting the restoration. Here again is a fine set of antique fireplace tiles. In the corner, a delicate Sheraton night stand from the Boston area (c. 1820) holds a Chinese carved soapstone pagoda.

The east parlor fireplace (opposite above) contains a complete set of puce delft tiles to match those in the west parlor. An English needlepoint pole screen, a Queen Anne easy chair, and a Sheraton mahogany settee from the Boston area (c. 1810) are grouped near the hearth.

The fruitwood settee in Chippendale style is probably Portuguese (opposite below). The English piano is by Astor and Co. (c. 1800). A walnut veneer blocked Dutch dressing table (c. 1725) stands between the windows.

The stair hall (right) is another example of the subtle interior of this house. The fine arch with carved keystone and brackets, and the spiral carvings of newel post and balusters all are in the great tradition.

The remarkable village of Old Deerfield, Massachusetts, is endowed with many historic houses, beautifully furnished. Our choice is the ASHLEY HOUSE, home of Jonathan Ashley, the village parson. Built before 1733, it has been restored in recent years. The most opulent room in the house is the parlor *(above)*. Its woodwork is painted a soft, lustrous blue. The settee is upholstered in rich yellow damask, and the Queen Anne easy chair is covered by magnificent American crewel on linen twill.

The famous Marble Chamber of the Royall House *(opposite above)* was and is one of the great rooms of the house. With marbleized and gilded pilasters, an overmantel portrait of the property, and choice old furniture from the Boston area, it remains unique.

The mahogany tall-case clock *(opposite above)* in the Marble Chamber is by Simon Willard *(c.*1800), and the bed is mahogany, Sheraton in style, from the Boston area. It is carved with acanthus leaves, festoons and flowers.

The central hallway of the Ashley House *(right)* is faced with thick vertical boards, paneled on both sides. The stairway is illuminated with what is known as a Paul Revere lantern. A Connecticut tall-case clock tells time in the corner.

The pine kitchen of the Ashley House *(above and opposite above)* is built in a salt-box lean-to and contains a fireplace of impressive dimensions. A most unusual carved paneled pine cupboard stands in one corner. Its shaped opening is framed with reversed scrolls. The kitchen fireplace is equipped with a clock-jack which turns the spit, and ample utensils to feed the parson's vigorous family of nine.

The parson's study *(opposite below)* is capably paneled, with enclosed cupboards flanking the fireplace. Two Pilgrim slat-back chairs sit primly before the fire. The rug is an antique Oushak.

A fine Connecticut carved sunflower chest reposes in the Ashley House *(right)*. On top is a Bristol delft posset cup flanked by two pewter Communion flagons from Connecticut.

The HUNTER HOUSE of Newport, Rhode Island, was probably an earlier house brought to its present state of formal beauty by changes and enlargements made for Deputy Governor Jonathan Nichols, Jr., a wealthy merchant, in 1748. The northeast parlor is a fine example of the style of the period in furniture and decoration.

The north bedroom of the Ashley House *(opposite above)* is conspicuous for its luxurious bed. Its hangings of richly colored crewelwork came from England. At the right is a Queen Anne dressing table fitted with an old courting mirror.

The south bedroom of the Ashley House *(opposite below)* is faced with unpainted sheathing, and simply furnished. This is the children's room with a trundle bed, but still rather inadequate for nine offspring.

A smaller reception room in the Hunter House is known as the Walnut Room because of floor-to-ceiling paneling which is painted to imitate walnut grain. The original fireplace tiles are Dutch, and the painting of two dogs above it is by, surprisingly enough, Gilbert Stuart *(right)*.

The upstairs northeast parlor of the Hunter House has a splendid architectural fireplace wall, similar in design to the room beneath it. The facing of the fireplace is painted to resemble marble. The arched shell cupboards with cherubim or angel heads in the spandrels, contain some Newport-owned porcelains.

The fireplace wall of the downstairs parlor of the Hunter House *(opposite above)* shows the marbleized Corinthian pilasters on their high pedestals. The shell cupboards are lined with a subtle green-blue paint, and the cherubim in the spandrels are colorfully and naturalistically painted. The splendid block-front desk is a Townsend-Goddard piece.

The keeping room at the back of the house *(opposite below)* contains a collection of early furniture and ornaments. The tall-backed, carved chairs are Carolean and William and Mary. The chest between the windows is seventeenth-century Flemish, and the wall clock is English (*c.*1675).

The dining-room woodwork *(left)* is painted in cedar graining, and the original Dutch fireplace tiles resemble those in the Walnut Room. The portrait is said to be of a member of the Townsend cabinet-making family.

The JOSEPH WEBB HOUSE in Wethersfield, Connecticut, was originally built in 1678, though the main or front portion of it dates from 1752. Here General Washington and the Comte de Rochambeau met and conferred for five days while planning the Yorktown campaign. Both parlors contain fine French papers and eighteenth-century furniture. One is carpeted with hooked rugs, and the other with semi-antique oriental carpets.

In the upstairs sitting room of the Hunter House, *(opposite)* a tall mahogany eighteenth-century desk-bookcase dominates one wall. It has ogee bracket feet and a shell-carved interior. The bold broken pediment and arched beveled panels are well related in strength and grace. The Queen Anne chair with turned stretchers has a colorful needlepoint seat.

The dining room of the Joseph Webb House contains a Hepplewhite sideboard and mirror, and some fine Chippendale chairs. Good pieces of silver and porcelain add lustre to the room.

A bedroom where George Washington actually did stay for several nights, and obviously the best chamber, reveals the quite astonishingly beautiful flock wallpaper hung in his honor just before his arrival (opposite above).

Upon entering the neighboring SILAS DEANE HOUSE, 1766 (opposite below), the visitor encounters a most lovely entrance hall with large panels and a well-lighted stairway with broad easy treads and carved spiral newel post and balusters.

The dining room of the Webb House (left) contains a handsomely designed mantelpiece. The curious arrangement of panels above reveals two small cupboards in the chimney. The house is owned and operated by the Connecticut Society of the Colonial Dames of America.

The furniture in the Chippendale Room of the Antiquarian House in Concord, Massachusetts, is of the Chippendale style as interpreted in a restrained New England way. The exception is the tall-backed American carved Carolean chair (c. 1685) which is placed here as an "heirloom". All furniture was Concord owned. The paneling is from a house in Salem, Massachusetts.

The LADY PEPPERELL HOUSE in the village of Kittery Point, Maine, (opposite above) was built in 1760. The dining-room floor is attractively painted to imitate black and white marble. Between the windows stands a Queen Anne lowboy. The mirror is Chippendale with a scrolled frame, and the portrait is of a member of the Waldron family by John Greenwood.

A view of one of the parlors (opposite below) shows the handsome recessed windows with interior shutters that obviated the need for hangings. The fireplace tiles are original, and the furniture comes from the middle and late eighteenth century.

The same parlor in the Lady Pepperell House (left) contains a tall Chippendale desk-bookcase with scrolled, hooded top, brass finials, and carved sunbursts, both in the top and interior compartment.

Sunshine pours into the southeast parlor of the DERBY HOUSE, the oldest brick house in Salem, Massachusetts. It was built in 1761–62 by Richard Derby, one of the town's most famous merchants, and reflects the early eighteenth-century style of architecture which he preferred. He built the house for his son, Elias Hasket Derby, who was equally celebrated. Sitting impressively at the head of the famous Derby Wharf, this historic house suffered from neglect and indifference until it was rescued by the Society for the Preservation of New England Antiquities. The old paneling was restored, and the original colors were matched in painting the interior. At present the Derby House is capably administered by the National Park Service, and is open to visitors. The southeast parlor *(above)* is furnished with early pieces, including a desk-on-frame from about 1700 and a bannister-back armchair. The woodwork is painted a rich olive green, while the bolection molding of the fireplace is painted a dull red in imitation of sandstone.

The southwest parlor *(opposite)* is similar in many ways, but it is furnished with more sophisticated pieces, among them a Queen Anne lowboy drop-leaf table, and an eighteenth-century easy chair.

The Derby House is furnished with some rare pieces, including this beautifully carved eighteenth-century desk-bookcase. Before it sits a simple turned corner chair.

The MOFFATT-LADD HOUSE in Portsmouth, New Hampshire, was built about 1763 by Captain John Moffatt as a wedding gift for his son, Samuel. It is a sumptuous mansion, flawlessly furnished. The drawing room *(above)* contains a fine Chinese Chippendale settee and armchair. Legend declares that the carvings on the mantelpiece were brought by John Moffatt from his home in England, and that they may be by Grinling Gibbons.

The scale of the elaborate central hall *(opposite above)* gives some indication of the way of life of a wealthy merchant's family of the time. The mansion and its handsome gardens are operated by the Society of the Colonial Dames of New Hampshire.

Fine paneling combined with a magnificent scenic paper called the "Vues d'Italie", or the Bay of Naples paper, decorates the central hall of the Moffatt-Ladd House *(opposite below)*, which is unique in America.

Looking down the great stair well, the visitor has a view of a dramatic section of the famous paper *(right)*, made by Joseph Dufour in Paris about 1815.

A niche in the dining-room wall of the Moffatt-Ladd House *(above)* holds the sideboard. The Georgian cornice and overmantel appear to be contemporary with the hall, while the mantelpiece and dado are of Federal style.

The JEREMIAH LEE MANSION at Marblehead, Massachusetts, was built in 1768 by one of the colonies' greatest merchant-shipowners. Lee had his great room *(opposite above)* paneled from ceiling to floor in pine carved with a great variety of moldings and magnificent relief decoration, conceived after English pattern book designs. The furniture is of the period.

A parlor of the Lee Mansion, arranged as a dining room *(opposite below)*, has a fine paneled fireplace wall with Corinthian pilasters and a fireplace opening framed with original tiles by Sadler and Green of Liverpool. The rug is an early English needlepoint. The mansion is owned by the Marblehead Historical Society, and is open during the summer months.

A bedroom of the Moffatt-Ladd House *(left)* contains a Hepplewhite field bed dressed with a netted canopy and a splendid old Trapunto linen counterpane.

The Lee Mansion entrance hall with stairs of majestic proportions is probably the most imposing in New England. Stairs and paneling are of Santo Domingo mahogany. A large Chippendale sofa stands against one wall, and a Simon Willard tall-case clock tells time at the far end.

A second floor drawing room *(opposite above)* has another of the impressive and individually designed chimney breasts found throughout the house. The famous English wallpaper, made expressly for these walls, is hand painted in tempera and depicts romantic scenes in rococo frames. Most of the furniture seen here is of the Queen Anne period.

The winter kitchen of the Jeremiah Lee Mansion *(opposite below)* is suitably furnished with comb-back and loop-back Windsor chairs, simple chests and a hutch table. The fireplace contains a weight-controlled spit of the period, and early utensils. The closet shelves hold a display of blue Staffordshire.

The carved chimney breast of the great room *(left)* is patterned after a design in Abraham Swan's book, *The British Architect or Builder's Treasury,* (London 1744–45, Plate 51).

An upper sitting room of the Lee Mansion is again handsomely paneled, this time with Ionic pilasters on high pedestals and a cushion molding above. The polychrome Sadler tiles are a very rare type. Here the wallpaper panels have subjects connected with the sea, honoring Jeremiah Lee's profession.

A bedroom *(left)* contains a splendid Hepplewhite bed of imposing proportions. A documented print has been used for the hangings and counterpane. The woodwork is painted an interesting olive green, reproduced from the original color.

The upper landing of the Jeremiah Lee Mansion as well as the stairway and the two front rooms of this floor retain the original English paper, the only set by this unknown maker still on the original walls in this country. The romantic subjects are taken from paintings and engravings by such eighteenth-century artists as Pannini, Vernet and Delafosse (trophies). The marble-topped Georgian sideboard-table bears a Chinese export bowl of immense proportions. Fine antique oriental carpets are found throughout the house.

On the upper landing, or hall, *(right)* is found a splendid bombé chest with original brasses, made in the area. The wall-paper panel depicting Roman ruins with figures in a rococo frame, is flanked by trophies after Delafosse. The paper is surrounded by a narrow paper border in egg-and-dart design which matches the carving on the door frames.

113

The NATHAN HALE HOMESTEAD in South Coventry, Connecticut, was erected in 1776 by the family of the great American patriot of the Revolution, some time after his death. Nathan Hale had grown up in an earlier house on this same land. The parlor *(above)* contains furniture of several periods, from the Queen Anne tea table to the Sheraton fancy chairs and an early pianoforte. Family memorabilia include the portrait of Nathan's brother, Major John Hale. This is one of the properties of the Antiquarian & Landmarks Society, Inc., of Conn.

The furniture of the farmhouse kitchen-dining room is of local origin. The fowling piece over the mantel was Nathan Hale's, and the pewter plates, copper kettles and dishes in the cupboard *(opposite above)* belonged to his sister Joanna.

The school room where Nathan Hale's brother David taught the neighborhood children *(opposite below)*, is fitted with celestial and terrestrial globes, a blackboard on the wall, school books and pens upon the table, and a brass bell.

The "best bedroom" *(left)* shows woodwork of considerable style. The space between the mantelpiece and cornice provides a perfect setting for a picture to complete this feature.

The HATHEWAY HOUSE in Suffield, Connecticut, is made up of a cluster of buildings of different periods, all somehow blended into a harmonious whole by the late eighteenth-century owner, Oliver Phelps. He really created the present glory of the mansion by installing the French wallpapers in the north wing which he had built about 1794. The parlor is a gem of the Federal style in woodwork, furniture, and one of the five French wallpapers shown above.

The whole original interior of the dining room, originally the parlor, *(opposite above)* has been transported to Winterthur Museum, which replaced it with perfect reproductions.

Another example of the hand-blocked papers decorates the large bedroom, *(opposite below)*. The borders in every case are an integral part of the original decor. Fluted corner piers are a feature of this room and the main parlor beneath it.

The stair hall *(left)* shows indications of the workmanship of about 1740, when the central portion of the house was built, especially in the Georgian paneling. Another of the French papers shows delicate neo-classic motifs in beautiful colors, with the borders intact.

Another bedroom in the Hatheway House *(above)* contains a delicate four-post bed, Sheraton fancy chairs, window hangings and French paper all in the Federal tradition.

The Revolutionary Bedroom in the ANTIQUARIAN HOUSE in Concord, Massachusetts, *(opposite above)* contains furniture of that period within its grey-blue paneled walls. The bed came from the Minot family of Concord, and the block-front chest of drawers between the windows is a Massachusetts piece, flanked by two country Chippendale chairs.

The Reeded Bedroom in the same Antiquarian House *(opposite below)*, takes its name from the early nineteenth-century decorative woodwork that was applied to mantels, dados and entablatures. The reeded post bed is well related to its setting. A reverse serpentine slant-top desk with ogee bracket feet and original brasses was made by Joseph Hosmer, Concord cabinet maker, as were other pieces in the room. The bed and window hangings are authentic *toile-de-Jouy* of the early nineteenth century.

Another view of the stair well of the Hatheway House shows a large area of neo-classical wallpaper with all the grace and delicacy of a Pompeian fresco.

118

Samuel McIntire, the famed architect and wood carver, was born in Salem, Massachusetts, in 1757, and designed most of his fine buildings for his native city. McIntire's father, a capable housewright, taught him the fundamentals of carpentry and wood carving, but the young man's ambition carried him much farther. He studied all the existing English books on classical architecture that he could find, and soon became the protégé of Elias Hasket Derby, foremost of Salem's merchant-shippers, as well as other prominent men. Among these was Jerathmeal Peirce, a wealthy shipper who commissioned McIntire, still in his twenties, to build a three-story mansion on Federal Street. The PEIRCE-NICHOLS HOUSE was the result of this assignment, and this early masterpiece, built in 1782, has often been characterized as the finest three-story house in New England. This was McIntire's Georgian style. The wood carving took many years to complete. Much later, in 1801, he remodeled the drawing room for the occasion of the marriage of Jerathmeal Peirce's daughter Sally to George Nichols, in his later, or Federal style. The west parlor of this house *(above)* is distinctly Georgian in feeling, and the moldings are deeply cut. A fine reverse-serpentine-front desk sits in a corner. The portraits are of an unknown lady and gentleman. In the hall *(left)* hangs a handsome gilt Chippendale mirror.

Samuel McIntire's gift for designing and carving woodwork is evident in this view of the upstairs sitting room of the Peirce-Nichols House. The Georgian mantel is framed by rich, heavy moldings, inside of which is imbedded a set of orange-red Sadler tiles. A delicate Sheraton sofa is placed near the fireplace. This is one of the four rooms in the house that have been restored and appropriately furnished, and opened to the public by the Essex Institute, present owner of the house.

A detailed view of the carving on this mantelpiece *(right)* gives an appreciation of McIntire's artistry as a woodcarver.

The superb mantelpiece of the drawing room of the Peirce-Nichols House is an example of McIntire's later Adamesque style of 1801. The mirror over the mantel was ordered from France at the time of Sally Peirce's wedding.

The drawing room is serene and dignified. The miniature upholstered sofas in the corners and four matching window seats were designed and built by McIntire for the wedding.

A detail of a doorway in the drawing room *(right)* reveals the extraordinary gift for graceful design and delicate carving possessed by the architect-carver of Salem.

The east bedroom of the Peirce-Nichols House is notable for its elaborate chimney breast, conceived in McIntire's Federal style. It introduces half-engaged columns and a panel of vertical reeding. Above it are framed two gouache paintings by the Neapolitan artist Michele Felice Cornè, whose work was widely received in Salem. The four-post bed in the foreground belonged to the Nichols family, as did the camphor-wood chest, leather covered and studded with brass nails.

Near the south window of this bedroom *(left)* is a superb old block-front mahogany chest-on-chest with shell carving, flanked by two Sheraton chairs.

The GOVERNOR JOHN LANGDON MANSION in Portsmouth, New Hampshire, was built by this much-travelled merchant-trader, Revolutionary patriot and politician who was five times elected governor of the state. Here, at the time of the French Revolution, he entertained Louis Phillipe and his brothers who had fled into exile. The house is furnished with English and American period pieces, a few of which belonged to Governor Langdon, as well as some suitable reproductions. The north parlor *(above)*, the scene of the Governor's receptions, is an indication of the Georgian style of the interior with dentiled cornice, Corinthian pilasters and broad arches with carved keystones which flank the ornately carved chimney breast. The room is furnished with dignity, and contains some fine oriental carpets.

The elaborate carving of the chimney breast of the north parlor *(right)* is a style found in other Portsmouth houses. Woodwork in the principal original rooms is painted in period grey and putty green.

A wing added in 1906 to the Governor John Langdon Mansion by McKim, Mead and White contains the octagonal dining room which is a copy of the one in the early house of Judge Woodbury Langdon, the Governor's brother. The original remains imbedded in the structure of the Rockingham Hotel in Portsmouth, which was constructed around the remaining parts of the judge's house. One of the china cupboards contains a lovely gold-banded set of porcelain used by the Langdons when entertaining President Washington in 1789.

The south parlor scenic paper *(opposite above)* is a reproduction. Here the same handsome Georgian woodwork is seen in cornice, dado and recessed windows.

The south parlor chimney breast *(opposite below)* is, like its counterpart in the north parlor, a provincial New Hampshire woodcarver's elaborate interpretation of Georgian designs. The pair of tall candle holders are notable.

The central stairway *(right)* is embellished by balusters in three patterns and a handsome newelpost carved in one piece, almost identical with the one in the Sarah Orne Jewett House in nearby South Berwick, Maine.

The HAMILTON HOUSE at South Berwick, Maine, was built in 1787 by Jonathan Hamilton, a descendant of early Scottish settlers in this region near Portsmouth, New Hampshire. He became a prosperous merchant-shipowner, and built his house and wharves at this beautiful site on a tidal river which was then navigable. Owners of the late nineteenth and early twentieth century did much to repair the old house, and left it in the hands of the Society for the Preservation of New England Antiquities, which has restored the rooms to their original colors and furnished them suitably. The northeast parlor *(above)* contains a number of painted and japanned pieces, including a painted Sheraton sofa and a japanned Chippendale desk and tall-case clock.

The southwest parlor of the Hamilton House *(opposite above)* has walls hung with paper painted with local scenes and historic landmarks in an earlier style, though done in the early twentieth century.

The spacious entrance hall *(opposite below)* is divided by a handsome arch, an example of the restrained Georgian architectural features of the house. A set of Chippendale ladder-back chairs is ranged along one wall.

The house was papered in 1898 *(right)* with an English copy of original pieces found under many layers on the wall. A ship model and a colorful painted chest add life and warmth to the setting.

In the Hamilton House's southwest parlor *(above)* the great architectural feature is the handsome chimney breast flanked by arches with carved soffits and keystones. A dentilled cornice, mahogany window seats, and folding shutters show fine craftsmanship. A three-backed Chippendale settee and a Queen Anne tea table are near the fireplace.

Two Martha Washington lolling chairs *(opposite above)* flank the simple, well-proportioned chimney breast, which extends into a bedchamber. A canopy bed with reeded posts is hung with old *toile-de-Jouy*.

The spacious southwest bedchamber *(opposite below)* has a pair of arches flanking the chimney, as in the parlor below. The Sheraton field bed has a netted canopy. A pair of colorful theorem paintings over the two chests of drawers make a balanced arrangement against the far wall.

The woodwork of the southwest parlor *(left)* is painted a pale grey-green. Harmonious against this tone are the ornaments on and near the mantelpiece, consisting of a Wedgwood black basalt bust of Washington, two Staffordshire "images" of Franklin and Chaucer, and a pair of graceful tripod pole screens.

The stately JOHN BROWN HOUSE in Providence, Rhode Island, was built for John Brown, philanthropist and merchant prince, in 1786. It was designed by his brother, Joseph Brown, and two years were needed to complete the massive three-story structure. John Quincy Adams called it "the most magnificient and elegant private mansion that I have ever seen on this continent." This view of a drawing room with arched doorways flanked by Ionic pilasters, and plaster-decorated ceiling, gives an idea of its Georgian splendor.

Elaborate carving of the mantelpiece, windows and cornices mark the interiors of the John Brown House *(above)*. This and other rooms on the ground floor are furnished with antique pieces of the period, and are open to visitors who apply. The house was presented to the Rhode Island Historical Society in 1936. George Washington visited the house in 1790, after his inauguration, and drank a glass of punch with his admirer, John Brown. The owner spent the last years of his life here from 1783 to 1803.

The central hallway of the house *(right)* gives an idea of its formality and splendor. Doorways with scrolled broken pediments lead to the side rooms, and classic busts repose on semi-detached columns with entablatures. The earlier Georgian architecture has become florid and somewhat impure. Federal motifs have begun to appear, such as the leaded sidelights surrounding the door.

The VALE at Waltham, Massachusetts, was the beautiful country estate of Theodore Lyman, successful Boston merchant, designed by Samuel McIntire of Salem, and completed in 1798. It was the home of the Lyman family for over a century and a half. It was surrounded by many acres of parkland and gardens, stables and outbuildings, and its greenhouses were famous. One can still see the wood-burning heating system, one of the oldest in the country, for growing exotic fruits and plants in a cold climate. The Bow Parlor *(above)* remains unchanged except for a slightly later classical mantelpiece. McIntire's *banquettes,* or window seats, and a pair of lacquered tables, one of which is seen at the left, have always been in this room. The painted Hepplewhite chairs and a set of Louis XVI chairs and settees also belonged to the Lyman family.

Samuel McIntire's ballroom *(opposite)*, with a coved ceiling and inspired use of classical columns, contains a Lyman family early pianoforte, and an Aubusson carpet in the foreground. Silhouetted against a far window is an interesting glass-backed fire screen in the shape of a lyre.

An early nineteenth-century mirror in the ballroom *(right)* reflects a glimpse of the fine classical marble mantelpiece and an early nineteenth-century portrait. Beneath the mirror stands an English Adamesque settee with painted decoration of musical instruments.

The JACOB WENDELL HOUSE was built in 1789 and though it has generally the solid Georgian character of the foregoing period, some Federal details appear, perhaps as later additions. On the parlor mantelpiece *(above)* is a pair of framed Chinese fans which belonged to members of the family. The gilded eagle is a fine piece of carving which, though contemporary, is based on early models. Eighteenth-century armchairs and a tall sideboard-table at left form part of the furnishings.

The simple dining room *(opposite above)* has exposed corner posts and solid inside shutters. The hatchment and coats of arms all have family connections. The Italian hand-painted window shade is contemporary, though the trophy design (emblems of the hunt) is inspired by eighteenth-century models.

A tall Sheraton bed *(opposite below)* has a tester valance and counterpane of colorful India print and a head curtain of crewelwork. The Sheraton painted settee is part of a set.

Woodwork in the study *(right)* approaches the Federal style in its more slender and delicate detail. A pair of Chippendale armchairs is near the fireplace. The silhouettes are likenesses of forebears of the owner.

137

An interesting historical restoration project came into being when Strawbery Banke Corporation combined with what had originally been an urban renewal project to rebuild the decayed area of the original settlement of Portsmouth, New Hampshire. The early settlement on the Piscataqua River (*c.*1630) took its name from the fields of wild strawberries found along its banks. The reconstruction project was launched in 1960. Much of the area was cleared. The best of the early buildings were saved, while others were moved in from other locations, including the Governor Ichabod Goodwin House (1811), illustrated on pages 171–173. The Chase House (1762), a fine representative of the mid-Georgian style, is shown here.

The rear parlor of the CHASE HOUSE *(above)* is furnished in pre-Revolutionary style with a fine Chippendale sofa upholstered in original needlepoint, and a tall desk-book-case with shell-carved interior and three flame finials.

The music room contains an early pianoforte *(opposite above)* and a pair of English Georgian ribband-back chairs. The formal window hangings and carefully detailed woodwork add dignity to the room.

The carving of the ample chimney-breast resembles others of this style in Portsmouth and is said to have been done by William Dearing the elder, a ship carver from nearby Kittery, Maine, who was born in 1706.

The dining room of the Chase House *(right)* contains a comfortable blend of a Queen Anne table, Chippendale chairs, and a Hepplewhite sideboard with a pair of family portraits above.

The reeded room of the Antiquarian House in Concord, *(above)* contains furniture of an earlier period. A reverse-serpentine chest of drawers is probably by Joseph Hosmer of Concord, as is the pair of country Chippendale chairs. The corner cupboard *(c.* 1725) and the fine fan-carved Queen Anne high chest are also Concord pieces.

The BARRETT HOUSE at New Ipswich, New Hampshire, *(opposite above)* was built shortly after 1800 by a prosperous owner of local cotton mills, and was owned by descendants until 1948. In it are represented several periods of family furniture from the eighteenth century to the Victorian period. The dining room contains a French scenic paper in full color by Zuber, (edition of 1836–37) from an old house in Quincy, Massachusetts. A set of Salem Hepplewhite chairs and a Chinese export porcelain service with sepia decoration complete the décor.

A bedroom in the Barrett House *(opposite below)* exhibits a later character in the very unusual Empire mahogany bureau with twisted columns, an attached dressing glass and original brasses. The fine porcelain urns on the mantelpiece are also Empire.

The reeded woodwork which gives the room its name is ex-emplified in this mantelpiece in the Antiquarian House *(left)*. The portrait is of Christopher Coates. He was known as the first calico printer in America.

GORE PLACE, the beautiful country estate of Christopher Gore (Harvard 1776) who later became Governor of Massachusetts (1809–10), was built in 1802–04. It is now believed that the architect was a Frenchman, and that Mrs. Gore, the former Rebecca Amory Paine, had much to do with the planning of her home. The spacious Music Room *(above)* has an exceptionally high ceiling, tall windows and delicate furniture which includes a Sheraton sofa, a pair of Gore family Sheraton fancy armchairs, and a Queen Anne tea table of infinite grace. The portrait is by Sir Joshua Reynolds.

The Empire parlor in the Barrett House *(opposite above)* is papered with a grey reproduction fashionable in the early nineteenth century. In the center is a pedestal Empire mahogany table with white marble top. The small sofa with swan-neck arms, Empire side chairs and window hangings draped in a pattern of the period, form a harmonious whole.

The northwest bedchamber of the Barrett House *(opposite below)* has window and bed hangings in a wine colored reproduction *toile* of a design by Huet called *Le Parc du Château* (c. 1783). The woodwork is a complementary soft green.

The graceful spiral stairway in Gore Place *(right)* soars upward from a marble-paved hall. The brass and glass lantern is English, *c.* 1790.

In the library of Gore Place *(above)* stands a tall Baltimore desk-bookcase, one of two large pieces containing books in this room. The Queen Anne game table holds a set of chess men.

The marble-paved State Reception Hall of Gore Place *(opposite above)* contains a large round table which belonged to Governor Gore, and a set of Chinese Chippendale chairs. Again the very high ceiling is noticeable, and a tall gilt Federal mirror rests over a beautiful classic mantel of the period.

A Federal mantelpiece in the State Reception Hall indicates the attention to fine detail observed throughout the mansion. A silver urn at the right rests upon a plate warmer of the period.

The main entrance to the marble-paved stair hall *(right)* shows the tracery of the beautiful fan light. Two Chinese porcelain garden seats and a tall-case clock, signed by Joachim Hill of New Jersey, ornament the area.

145

The study with an oval shape in Gore Place is directly above the oval dining room. This was Governor Gore's office while he was serving as chief executive, and reflects the fashion of that time in Sheraton and Empire furniture.

Mrs. Gore's spacious light bedchamber (below) contains a four-post Hepplewhite bed of mammoth proportions with a fretted tester. The portrait over the fireplace is by Joseph Badger.

The Oval Room, now the dining room at Gore Place *(opposite)* is papered with a copy of the original paper found on these walls. A fine Federal mantel, a circular convex mirror, large Chinese jars and a French crystal *lustre* ornament the room. A silver mirrored plateau which belonged to Mrs. Gore's family centers the Philadelphia Sheraton table.

The GARDNER-PINGREE HOUSE in Salem, Massachusetts, considered the finest brick house designed by Samuel McIntire, was built for Captain John Gardner in 1804. It was acquired by David Pingree in the 1830's and remained in the Pingree family for decades until it was turned over to the Essex Institute. Under this ownership it has been restored, flawlessly furnished, and opened to the public. Samuel McIntire's finest wood carving was reserved for this house. One famous mantelpiece motif was the decorative oval fruit basket *(above)* which appears in the front parlor. Another was the delicate wheat sheaf, which became something of a McIntire symbol. Some of the repeat patterns, as those on the cornices, are composition cast from wooden molds carved by McIntire. In the Victorian era, some of the McIntire wooden mantels were replaced by marble ones, considerably more in the taste of the times. Luckily the originals were found stored in the attic, and have been restored to their former setting.

The front parlor of this house *(left)* shows a well-lighted Chippendale card table surrounded by four Hepplewhite chairs. The pair of tall candle stands are very choice. The unsymmetrical window hangings are made of fine India mull with "tambour" embroidery.

The front and back parlors of this remarkable house have almost identical fireplaces. This one is in the front, and two orange-yellow Chinese export urns lend it distinction. Above it is a panel of an old French wallpaper, designed by Fragonard *fils* in 1808. Each panel represents a different month of the year.

Study of the mantelpiece of the rear parlor of the Gardner-Pingree House reveals Samuel McIntire in an ornate mood. The half-engaged columns are strung with garlands, and the moldings are richly decorated. A Chinese export garniture of porcelain vases ornaments the mantel.

The wheat sheaf *(opposite)* is the most personal of McIntire's carved devices, and nothing better proves his mastery of the chisel. This example is from the mantel of the Crowninshield room.

The dining room of this house *(right)* is painted a simple turquoise blue. Surrounded by eight Sheraton chairs, the table is set with a silver mirrored plateau holding a handsome candelabrum. The portrait over the sideboard is one of a pair by Blackburn.

151

The northeast bedchamber of the Gardner-Pingree House is a study in balance. A Chippendale mirror hangs over the serpentine-front chest of drawers. The mantelpiece, carved with restraint, is brightened by blue delft jars. Nearby is a painted candle screen.

A gilded girandole mirror of ambitious scale hangs in the hallway and reflects the main staircase *(left)*. It is ornamented with foliage, a pair of curvaceous dolphins and an eagle on a high perch.

152

The southwest bedchamber, known as the Francis Shaw Memorial room, is painted a robin's egg blue. Above the simple mantel is a gilt-framed Salem mirror, flanked by two Bartolozzi English mezzotints and fine crystal candelabra which belonged to Elias Hasket Derby. The chairs are in the French Chippendale style (probably English) with Chinese backs. A Martha Washington armchair sits by the hearth. The window and bed hangings are made of a copy of eighteenth-century French brocaded silk, in blue with small red roses. A Seymour chest of drawers with a dressing glass is visible at the left.

The "marriage bed" in the Crowninshield Memorial bedroom *(right)* is most colorful, being hung with blue and apricot damask. The corner washstand has Chinese export porcelain fittings.

A glimpse of the hallway of the Gardner-Pingree House shows two of McIntire's doorways carved with his wheat sheaves, and a portion of his very individual staircase. The original stair balustrade had been replaced by a Victorian one in the later nineteenth century. Some pieces of what was considered the original were found and put back in place with copies to complete the balustrade. A Chinese lantern hangs above.

The GRAY HOUSE in Massachusetts, *(above)* was built in 1808 and displays the style of the Federal period in its architectural details such as modillioned cornices, the dado trim, tall doors with entablatures above and delicate decoration in the architraves. The mantelpieces also have these characteristic carved and molded classical motifs. The library has such a mantel, surmounted by an English Chippendale gilded looking-glass, a particularly charming painted French Directoire screen in the corner, and a pair of Louis XVI armchairs with original needlepoint covering in strong and rich colors.

In the library of the Gray House *(right)* a very fine painting of the Post-Impressionist school, by Franklin C. Watkins, hangs above the sofa.

The dining room of the Gray House *(above)* has silk damask hangings of a soft, warm apricot shade. The walls are of the same color and the Spanish rug is toned to harmonize with them. The chairs are Chippendale. Between the windows hangs a clock by Lemuel Curtis, of Concord.

The parlor of the Gray House *(opposite above)* is decorated in tones of soft apricot and blue. Louis XV side chairs, an English eighteenth-century sofa "in the French taste" with matching side chairs and a Regency velvet-covered stool are most harmonious together. The wall clock is marked "S. Willard – Patent".

The wide, inviting entrance hall *(opposite below)* is paved with golden yellow marble, leading to the graceful spiral staircase and a garden door. The break-front low cabinet on the right is English. Above it hangs an English Chippendale looking-glass, and on the left stands a pair of painted English Adamesque tables. Crystal sconces glow on plain painted walls.

In the dining room *(left)* the simple cornice and dado are reeded, and the mantelpiece is decorated with a classical Greek lamp design and leafy garlands. The painting above is an eighteenth-century scene of Roman ruins of the romantic school.

The parlor of the NICKELS-SORTWELL HOUSE at Wiscasset, Maine, contains simple furnishings of two centuries from a Chippendale armchair to an Empire sofa. On the mantel is a pair of astral lamps and above it a local ship's portrait.

The RUNDLET-MAY HOUSE, built in New Hampshire by James Rundlet in 1805 is still owned by descendants and furnished completely with family pieces. Though the house is generally Federal in style, the handsome window on the stair landing expresses a feeling of the preceding Georgian tradition. The wall clock is by Lemuel Curtis. Nearby hangs a family portrait.

The bedchamber of the Rundlet-May House (*above*) contains a Sheraton field bed with netted canopy, a Hepplewhite chest of drawers with beautifully grained, veneered drawer panels, and a Federal looking-glass above it. The room has the cool, uncluttered charm of northern New England interiors.

The unusual parlor mantel shows the wood carving of a skillful craftsman. The very slender colonnettes at the corners are seldom seen. Nearby are two of a set of Sheraton fancy chairs with a bow and quiver of arrows motif in the splat.

The RUGGLES HOUSE in Columbia Falls, Maine, was built for Thomas Ruggles, the lumber king of this small village, in about 1817. The restrained and gracious parlor *(above)* expresses its owner's desire for a fitting residence in the most fashionable Federal style while still containing it within modest proportions. The result is a charming mansion in miniature, fine in design and embellished with some of the most skillful and intricate wood carving of this period in New England. Ruggles family pieces have been retrieved wherever possible to help furnish the rooms. Here the mirror and two lyre-backed chairs belong to this category. Off-white woodwork, soft green window hangings and golden upholstery are flattering to the little Federal parlor.

The divided freestanding staircase *(left)* is an unexpected and impressive feature of the house, a sophisticated piece of construction for a small village.

The colonnettes and panels of the chimney piece of the Ruggles House *(opposite)* are in natural mahogany, some with inlays, contrasting with the off-white painted woodwork. Details include reeding, garlands, and other classic motifs as well as the carver's petal-like forms of the capitals. These gently curved motifs were the carver's own creation, occuring in the capitals of the upper colonnettes and in other places inside and outside the house. Rarely has such exquisite carving been seen in New England.

The west bedchamber in the Ruggles House contains a number of pieces that were originally possessions of the Ruggles family. They include the pretty arched canopy Hepplewhite bed, a country Empire desk between the windows, the comb-back Windsor chair, spinning wheel and musket. The netted canopy, the patchwork quilt, beautifully worked, knit and fringed counterpane, the hooked and braided rugs, all bespeak country handcrafts at their thrifty best; fresh and charming and typically State-of-Maine.

The dining room *(left)*, originally a second parlor, contains a simpler example of the same style of woodwork as that seen in the parlor. Inset panels of contrasting wood decorate the chimney piece with a pinwheel and a type of bellflower design. The dining room chairs are lyre-backed within a type of Chippendale frame, probably English. The child's chair matches a set of Ruggles family Empire chairs in the room.

The DESHON-ALLYN HOUSE stands in the grounds of the Lyman Allyn Museum in New London, Connecticut. It was built in 1829 and is furnished with late Federal and Empire pieces suitable to its time. Many of these belonged to the Deshons and the Allyns. The north parlor, or music room, contains a New York pianoforte by W. Geib, and an Erard harp made in London in 1832. The music stand with brass candle brackets is also English, and the mahogany Empire side chairs (*c.*1830) are part of a set which was in the house originally.

Another view of the north parlor *(right)* shows an imposing nine-foot mahogany Empire secretary attributed to Joseph Meeks and Sons of New York. The winged eagle brackets above the paw feet are striking examples of Empire carving, as are those on the small Empire sofa at the left, where dolphins form the frontal curve of the arms. The French crystal chandelier comes from a nearby estate.

The south parlor of the Deshon-Allyn House shows the Empire influence, but tempered with New England restraint. The Grecian couch is painted black and gold, and is probably English Regency. The gilded mirror is Empire, and the marble bust was done in Rome in 1853 by Chauncy B. Ives. The card table between the windows and the chairs, however, harks back to the Sheraton style. The portrait by Isaac Sheffield of New London is of Captain John Bolles, descendant of a family that once lived on these acres.

The upper hall is illuminated by a charming leaded Palladian window, an example of how New Englanders clung to their favorite neo-classical style, when many others had turned to the Greek Revival. Empire influence appears in the charming furnishings, however, as in the four swan-neck arms of the little mahogany bench, and the sturdy brass-mounted columns of the chest at the left.

The dining room of the Deshon-Allyn House suggests the rather stolid comfort of the times, where large and heavy meals were served in a background of polished mahogany, marble mantels and family portraits, in this case one of Captain Lyman Allyn. A painted tôle plate warmer stands near the hearth. The curious sideboard near the door is a Connecticut country piece, ornately carved and naïvely designed.

The upper hall *(right)* is decorated with distinctive touches of the period, such as the two-toned woodwork and the Greek frieze border of the paper. The handsome gilded Empire pier glass is attributed to Isaac Platt of New York. The pier table *(c.*1830) is mahogany with a white marble top and columns with gilt bronze mounts. It has gilded carved feet and a mirror back reflecting a Wedgwood wine cooler. Other ornaments are Italian marble obelisks and a French *faïence* compote.

The VASSALL-CRAIGIE-LONGFELLOW HOUSE in Cambridge, Massachusetts, was built in 1759 by Henry Vassall, a member of a wealthy family of Jamaica planters who left New England at the time of the Revolution. The house was Washington's headquarters for nearly a year. It later became the property of Andrew Craigie, whose widow in 1837 rented rooms to Henry Wadsworth Longfellow. After he married Fanny Appleton of Boston they became owners of the house, which is now maintained in his memory, furnished as he left it. The study *(above)* was where he worked, and contains such memorabilia as a portrait of the poet painted by his son Ernest, a bust by Thomas Crawford in front of the mirror, and a portrait of Nathaniel Hawthorne in an oval frame at the left. The turkey red curtains with black velvet bands were hung in 1872.

In the west parlor, against the flowered wallpaper, stands a French clock under glass, purchased by Mrs. Longfellow in 1836 in Paris before her marriage. It rests upon a Gothic bracket shelf that she purchased for it in 1843. The pair of Bohemian red glass bottles fit into separate vase-shaped bases.

The great Georgian chimney breast of 1759 has a broken pediment, strong dentils, Corinthian pilasters and a white, grey-veined marble mantel. It looks down unmoved upon Longfellow's Victorian parlor. With deeply recessed arches at each side, it forms a handsome architectural wall.

Above the rococo revival sofa hangs a large painting of the grandchildren of Sir William Pepperell of Kittery, Maine.

The original kitchen had been converted into a dining room by the Craigies in the late eighteenth century, at which time the green marble mantel was installed. The mahogany Empire table and chairs and other furnishings were all Longfellow possessions.

The Longfellows' son, Charles Appleton Longfellow, lived for a time in China and Japan, which accounts for the many oriental objects in the house, including this red and gold lacquered table, the Chinese porcelains upon it and the pair of Japanese *cache-pots* below. The painting above is by Theodore Buchanan Read, done in 1859, and is the combined portraits of Longfellow's little daughters, "Grave Alice, and laughing Allegra and Edith with golden hair" made famous in *The Children's Hour*.

The GIBSON HOUSE, Boston, Massachusetts. In 1859 Mrs. Charles Hammond Gibson built one of the first houses in the Back Bay at 137 Beacon Street. It was the home of this family for three generations until left, endowed, as a public museum. This large bedroom contains a complete set of "bamboo" furniture, including a huge bed, divided dressing table, chests of drawers, night table and little tufted chairs. Its curtains and upholstery are the original floral printed cretonne. At the left is a foot bath of Mason's Ironstone ware.

The GOVERNOR GOODWIN MANSION in Portsmouth, New Hampshire, (opposite above) was built in 1811, and after a number of changes of ownership came into the hands of Ichabod Goodwin, Governor of the State from 1859–61. He lived in the house until he died in 1882. It still contains original Federal features as well as Greek revival and Civil War period changes made by the Governor. Many of the furnishings are gifts of a descendant. The Greek revival-Victorian parlor was once the Governor's office.

In the dining room (opposite below) the black marble mantel and coal-burning grate are the Governor's early Victorian installations. The chromo-lithograph, a still life of fruit, is a fitting dining room piece.

The dark woodwork of the stair hall of the Gibson House (left) shows the Renaissance revival influence of this Victorian period. The red stair carpet, the wall covering which imitates embossed Spanish leather, the pier table and the ornaments are all original with the house.

In the Governor Goodwin mansion the parlor mantel is of white marble with carved anthemion designs of the Greek revival period. The windows are framed with Victorian woodwork, including hollow-paneled pilasters with leaves of Egyptian character in the capitals.

The Federal woodwork remains unchanged in this room *(opposite above)*, though the square pianoforte, sofa, mirror and side chairs are Empire.

A central table of the Eastlake period *(opposite below)* and the what-not and high backed chairs with curves of the rococo revival style all mark these furnishings as belonging to Governor Goodwin's time.

The mahogany dining room sideboard *(right)* is typical of the Empire period, with twisted columns, overhanging drawers and lion head brasses with rings for handles. A crystal chandelier with hurricane shades matches the one in the parlor.

Of the many extraordinary houses in Newport, Rhode Island, we have chosen KINGSCOTE as a striking example of Victorian Gothic. Designed by Richard Upjohn and built in 1841, it is a fine example of the *cottage orné* that was popular at that time. It is modest in scale compared to most Newport summer houses. The double parlor, one end of which is shown above, is graced by two fine Gothic archways and furniture of many origins, French, Victorian and Oriental. Many of the Chinese pieces are from the collection of the second owner, who traded with China in the nineteenth century.

The stair hall in Kingscote *(left)* is brightened by Chinese porcelains. The trefoil decoration of the wainscot panels is deeply carved. An ornate carved octagonal Italian table and an eighteenth-century tall-case clock add further interest.

The dining room of Kingscote *(opposite above)* was designed by Stanford White as a very young man in 1880–81. It is astonishingly contemporary in the modern idiom. Some of the walls are wainscoted, but at the end, flanking a huge fireplace, are walls made of glass brick. Cork inlay covers the upper walls and ceiling.

The library fireplace *(right)* is carved with fine Gothic detail. A Chinese carved fire screen with a painted porcelain center stands in the fireplace opening. Above the mantel is a portrait of the Chinese agent and friend of American traders, Houqua, attributed to Chinnery.

ROSELAND COTTAGE in the village of Woodstock, Connecticut, is one of the more recent acquisitions of the Society for the Preservation of New England Antiquities. This Gothic Revival mansion was built in 1846 as a summer home for Henry Chandler Bowen, a prosperous Brooklyn publisher *(The Independent)* and a native of this village. The architect was Joseph C. Wells. The exterior paint of pink with dark red trim is as fresh as ever, and the interior is in a remarkable state of preservation. It still retains the original furniture designed for it. The front and back parlors of Roseland Cottage are identical in plan, and each has a deep bay window. The front parlor *(above)* shows a typical nineteenth-century arrangement with a marble-topped octagonal pedestal table and two flanking chairs, one of them part of the Gothic set designed for the house. The Italian carved mantel carries a set of bronze and crystal candelabra.

A bulging sideboard *(left)* with heavily carved brackets supporting two marble shelves, lends an air of opulence to the dining room.

Henry Chandler Bowen, the original owner of Roseland Cottage, was a philanthropist and an attentive host. He gave Roseland Park to the village of Woodstock in 1876, and later inaugurated the Fourth of July celebrations that became famous because of the celebrated speakers that Bowen brought to the platform. The rear parlor of Roseland Cottage *(above)* is illuminated by frosted diamond-shaped panes of red, blue, gold, green and violet set in mullioned casements. The light comes through in rainbow-like diaper patterns. The Gothic settee, especially designed for the house, compels attention.

The Gothic-arched passage between the front and back parlors is deep enough to contain two closets and two sliding doors. The doors and soffits are grained to simulate live oak. The gilded eagle that once topped the flagpole on the lawn has come to rest here. The heavily embossed wallpaper in both parlors is dark green on a cream colored ground. Known as Lincrusta, it was created to resemble the earlier Spanish leather. This was made in England in the 1860's.

VICTORIA MANSION in Portland, Maine, built between the years of 1859–63, is considered unsurpassed among museum houses as an example of high style Victorian architecture, especially since it contains a large proportion of its original furnishings. It was rescued from being demolished to make way for a service station, and is now maintained by the Victoria Society of Maine Women which makes it available to visitors during the summer months. The "French" drawing room or parlor *(above)*, completed in 1863 by architect Henry Austin, contains a rich assortment of decorative details. Numerous *amorini*, or cherubim, appear in painted medallions on walls and ceiling, as well as on the marble mantel, mirror frame and chandelier. Gold leaf, damask hangings and masses of roses, both painted and woven in the magnificent carpet, contribute to the rich effect. Furnishings include a Steinway concert grand and a black satin tufted *chaise longue*.

Charming small tufted satin side chairs, an elaborately carved Italian rosewood table, and vases and ornaments original with the house are included in this drawing room *(left)*.

The well of a mahogany flying staircase rises for three floors, illuminated by a pair of bronze torch bearers on the newel posts, and a sensational chandelier suspended from the roof and carrying two clusters of lamps at different levels. Austin's ornate gilded brackets support the second floor gallery.

The dining room of Victoria Mansion is paneled in hand carved chestnut and contains a French clock, especially designed to be a permanent part of the mantelpiece. The pair of massive carved serving tables match the sideboard (not shown) and display pieces of Portland glass (1804–73). The punch bowl was originally in the house.

The music room of Victoria Mansion *(left)* is also decorated in the lavish style inspired by the French (and Italian) Renaissance, featuring such details as gilt masks, urns, garlands of fruits and ribbons, classic pediments and cartouches. The heavy fringes and tassels on the window draperies, as well as the tie-backs, are original. Pretty little tufted chairs in turquoise damask, a tufted wine-red satin, circular seat surmounted by a marble group, and a most unusual square rosewood piano with mother-of-pearl keys and inlay, are featured here. The piano was a gift from former Maine Governor and Mrs. William Tudor Gardiner.

A CHARLESTON HOUSE, in Massachusetts, and unique in New England, is a brick residence especially constructed in 1923 to contain the woodwork of four large rooms of Adamesque style that were rescued from demolition in Charleston, South Carolina. The railway company was about to tear down the old mansion, dating from about 1800, woodwork, mantels and all, but a perceptive New Englander stepped in and bought all the best paneling, doorways and windows, and shipped everything of value north by schooner during World War I. Using old brick rescued from a nearby factory, the house was built around four paneled rooms, with added accommodations on a second floor and in a kitchen wing. The hall shown above contains the Charleston staircase, wide arch, architectural door frames and dado, and is papered with an English paper of Chinese design dated about 1760. The painted cabinet on the right is Venetian.

In the hall of this house *(right)* stands an English table by William Kent, and above it hangs an early sixteenth-century Spanish altarpiece. The beautifully harmonious eclecticism of the owner's collection includes here also a Chien Lung vase and a pair of English Sheraton armchairs.

The transplanted Charleston house has an ample drawing room with two desk-bookcases. The one on the right was made early in the twentieth century and carries in the pediment an eagle said to have been carved by Samuel McIntire of Salem. The eighteenth-century piece on the left also has carving attributed to the carver architect of Salem. English Adam ornaments frame the door and Louis XVI chairs with a matching settee form a group on the right.

The drawing room *(left)* shows the fine Charleston woodwork to advantage. The crystal chandelier came from an old Boston residence. A Bilbao mirror hangs above the mantelpiece, and both rugs are Karabagh.

The "Angel's Room" in the Charleston house is so called because of the delightful group of Spanish Polychrome carvings which surround the fifteenth-century Hispano-Flemish altarpiece over the fireplace. This room also contains a delicately carved Charleston cornice and dado, and fine putty mold decoration on the mantelpiece. Italian walnut armchairs, a Spanish table bearing a small French alabaster Virgin from Savoy, an elaborately carved hardwood chest of Eastern origin (possibly Indian), and a Kilim carpet contribute to its beauty. The chandelier matches the one in the drawing room.

The dining room *(right)* contains a Robert Adam sideboard designed by him for Kenwood House in England.

A graceful architectural doorway from the Charleston, South Carolina house *(overleaf)* frames a view of the Angel's Room.

INDEX